YOUR COMPANION
TO
12 STEP RECOVERY

■

YOUR COMPANION
TO
12 STEP RECOVERY

■

Robert Odom

Hay House, Inc.
Carson, CA

Published and distributed in the United States by:

Hay House, Inc.
1154 E. Dominguez St.
P.O. Box 6204
Carson, California 90749-6204

Edited by: Jill Kramer
Typesetting and internal design by: Freedmen's Typesetting
  Organization, Los Angeles, CA 90004

Library of Congress Cataloging-in-Publication Data

Odom, Robert.
    Your companion to 12 step recovery / Robert Odom.
        p.   cm.
    Includes bibliographical references.
    ISBN 1-56170-098-3 (pbk.)
    1. Twelve-step programs—Meditations.   2. New thought.
3. Spiritual life.   I. Title.
BL624.5.036   1994
291.4'4—dc20   94-10243
                                                      CIP

ISBN 1-56170-098-3

99 98 97 96 95   5 4 3 2 1
First Printing, June 1994

Printed in the United States of America
on recycled paper

This book is dedicated to

George Harrison,

whose musical prasad

has enriched us all.

Jai Guru Deva, OM*

*This prayer/mantra honors the Divine Wisdom that blesses us and transforms our material world activities into Spiritual awareness.

Contents

APPENDIX

Preface

The past decade has witnessed an explosion of interest in the 12 Steps, along with an even greater interest in self-empowerment through metaphysics and New Thought philosophies. Having been involved with 12 Step recovery programs since the 1970s and with metaphysics even longer, I became aware of the need to balance these influences in my spiritual development. I went from bookstore to bookstore looking for a meditation manual or even a pamphlet that might help those of us in recovery whose spirituality was metaphysically oriented. I couldn't find anything remotely helpful, so I went home and wrote this book you now hold in your hands.

The process of writing has added depth to my recovery and spiritual awareness. I hope it will to yours, as well.

I have tried to "keep it simple." This book is intended as a companion to 12 Step recovery, not as a substitute for it.

I have included a glossary where I've given my own definitions of commonly used metaphysical and 12 Step recovery terms. I especially had fun with this section—writing about complicated, multifaceted concepts in just a few sentences.

Finally, I listed some books that have proved invaluable to my own recovery and spiritual quest. These books are my good friends, and I visit them often. From a personal standpoint, I believe you will find anything written by Ram Dass, Louise Hay, or Stuart Wilde to be helpful on the journey of self-empowerment and personalized recovery.

If you find yourself working on a Step and not enjoying yourself, put it aside for a while and do something else. You can always return to it later. The Steps are not meant to be torturous. There is an inner timing in recovery that we always do well to acknowledge.

Trust your Higher Self to guide you through the initial recovery process into your own personal Knowing.

I am confident that you will want to keep a written record of working the Steps, especially your Fourth Step. This written record of your recovery will prove useful later on as you begin to share your experience, strength, and hope with others. Use the activities offered in chapters 1 to 12 of this book to record your recovery, and use your journal as well. Discovering that you have become an "oldtimer" is one of the wonderful surprises that recovery offers. These unexpected twists and turns are amazing.

I honor you as a fellow pilgrim on the journey of Recovery and Self-Discovery.

If you have fun reading this book, my purpose in writing it will have been achieved.

Walk in balance and harmony.

Robert Odom
Santa Fe, New Mexico
1994

Acknowledgements

I would like to thank the following for their love, encouragement, and support:

All my clients who teach me so much: James Efferson; Buffy, Sissy and Jodie Marie; Nancy Callahan; Seborn Ransom Odom and Princess; Charlene Bigham and James Allison; Wendy Moss; Louise Hay and the staff at Hay House (especially Jill Kramer, who has been my Guardian Angel through the editing and publication process of this book); and most special thanks to Red Sand Coyote.

THE TWELVE STEPS OF
ALCOHOLICS ANONYMOUS

1. We admitted we were powerless over alcohol—
that our lives had become unmanageable.

2. Came to believe that a Power greater than ourselves could restore us to sanity.

3. Made a decision to turn our will and our lives over
to the care of God, *as we understood Him.*

4. Made a searching and fearless moral inventory of
ourselves.

5. Admitted to God, to ourselves, and to another human being the exact nature of our wrongs.

6. Were entirely ready to have God remove all these
defects of character.

7. Humbly asked Him to remove our shortcomings.

8. Made a list of all persons we had harmed, and became willing to make amends to them all.

9. Made direct amends to such people wherever possible, except when to do so would injure them or
others.

10. Continued to take personal inventory and when we
were wrong promptly admitted it.

11. Sought through prayer and meditation to improve our conscious contact with God *as we understood Him,* praying only for knowledge of His will for us and the power to carry that out.

12. Having had a spiritual awakening as the result of these steps, we tried to carry this message to alcoholics, and to practice these principles in all our affairs.

The Twelve Steps are reprinted with permission of Alcoholics Anonymous World Services, Inc. Permission to reprint and adapt the Twelve Steps does not mean that A.A. has reviewed or approved the contents of this publication nor that A.A. agrees with the views expressed herein. A.A. is a program of recovery from alcoholism—use of the Twelve Steps in connection with programs and activities which are patterned after A.A., but which address other problems, does not imply otherwise.

Chapter 1

Step One: An Honest Beginning

"WE ADMITTED WE WERE POWERLESS OVER ALCOHOL—THAT OUR LIVES HAD BECOME UNMANAGEABLE."

Recovery begins the very moment you have the desire to stop self-destructive behavior and believe, if only for a moment, that such a thing is possible for you. People who have dealt with addictions to alcohol, food, drugs, or religion become very knowledgeable about pain. They have also become very creative in dealing with life through the fog of addiction. It amazes me how much talent and creativity can be manifested by a using addict. Of course, this creativity is often brought forth as cheating or lying! If we only could realize, in the midst of all that pain, that relief can be as close as the next moment. There is not only hope, but infinite promise and possibility, when you release the need to orchestrate life from the limited arena of addiction.

I believe that addiction can be the fertile ground from which our spiritual awareness grows. It is one of the supreme cosmic ironies that the things we view as curses—that is, alcoholism, eating disorders, drug addictions, and so on, so often turn out to be the very avenues that bring us to self-awareness, self-acceptance, and spiritual enlightenment. Spirit truly has a sense of humor.

I am also convinced that our primary orientation is toward Spirit, or the Good. Despite all the evidence to the contrary, I believe people want to be well, whole, and complete. Now, if this is true, why is there so much pain connected with addiction? The answer is really quite simple. Every drinking alcoholic, every using addict, every overeating or undereating compulsive eater, anyone in the clutches of an addiction, is seeking happiness and a feeling of safety.

No one picks up a drink and says, "Okay, now I'll become an alcoholic! I'll wreck my car and all my relationships. I'll lose my job and my home and eventually die a painful death!"

No one gorges themselves on food, or purges or starves themselves, saying, "Well, I'll completely destroy my physical health and watch my body disintegrate!" Far from it. People in the midst of their addictions are looking for some relief from their pain.

12 Step Programs

Thank goodness there are 12 Step programs to deal with addictions. One of the hallmarks of the New Age is the strong impulse toward self-empowerment, and helping others who share the same issues. This really began back in the 1920s with the original founders of Alcoholics Anonymous (A.A.). I believe they were prophets of Spirit. They challenged the medical establishment, many members of whom had given up on alcoholics. They offered hope where little or none had existed before. May Spirit bless them all!

However, over the years, as more and more people became involved in recovery, the "program" got codified. Rather than delve too deeply into that area, let me simply state the following: Recovering people who did not share traditional Judeo-Christian tenets became more and more uncomfortable simply identifying themselves by an addiction. Stating: "I am an alcoholic" ceased being liberation from denial; rather, it became extremely limiting.

Those of us who have worked with daily affirmations and meditation have become aware of just how powerful our words are. We have become more and more careful about making "I AM" statements.

On a personal level, I began seeking ways of expressing my recovery that did not limit my possibilities. I found others who shared my concerns, and soon I was teaching classes and workshops about metaphysical recovery. I went from bookstore to bookstore, searching in vain for a metaphysical meditation book on the Steps. Finally, I just wrote one!

What Is Metaphysical Spirituality?

Metaphysical Spirituality, which provides much of the basis for the material in this book, encourages individuals to explore relationships to Spirit only in ways that are supportive and empowering. It allows our individual interests and tastes to be part of a spiritual journey. In Metaphysical Spirituality, we are free to move beyond traditional restraints of religion, ethnicity, race, nationality, and so on. There are any number of avenues to explore as an individual of power. But remember, it really takes dedication and belief in yourself to step out of the crowd.

For example, in metaphysics, you can discover very ancient spiritual wisdom that may not be a part of the tradition into which you were born. The genuine traditions are always willing to share their wisdom; however, the more politicized people are, the less willing they are to share their spirituality.

Metaphysical Spirituality allows us to move beyond petrified institutions and refresh our approach to Spirit. It encourages us to move beyond our comfort zones and step out into an arena that allows and nourishes creativity. It must always leave room for individual interests and differences and resist becoming codified. This impulse toward individual creativity can keep recovery exciting and open to interdimensional exploration. This freedom can greatly enhance the pleasure you reap from your recovery.

Now, I do not envision my interpretation as a replacement for traditional recovery, nor do I presume that my metaphysical beliefs are "The Way." I do know, though, that Metaphysical Spirituality is very compatible with the 12 Steps.

The Complexity of the Ego-Self

You see, we all have personalities, and these personalities are made up of various components that I call "ego-selves." For example, we have an "inner-child ego-self," an "adolescent ego-self," a "competent adult ego-self," and those of us who have addictions also have an "addicted ego-self." The latter is that part of us that winds up addicted to people, places, or things that keep it from feeling scared or vulnerable. So, rather than having us go insane, our addicted ego-self tries to save us!

Now, after a while, things really get messy because the addiction takes on a life of its own. When I was able to let the responsibility for my addiction rest on my "addicted ego-self," I began to enjoy my recovery. I no longer had to do daily battle with a "disease."

I AM a man of power. I AM a part of the Spiritual Force that creates this universe. Also, I have an ego-self that is addicted to alcohol and food. That ego-self would prefer to drink mimosas and eat fried foods all day long! That ego-self is an alcoholic and a compulsive eater. But that is not who I AM! It is only a part of my personal history in this particular lifetime. I believe I have lived many lifetimes before this one, so I AM statements are crucial to what I manifest in my life now. I refuse to define my "self" by any disability.

For me to say, "I am an alcoholic," would be akin to saying, "I am nearsighted," or "I am a sore finger." It felt so liberating the moment I was able to acknowledge my alcoholism without *defining* myself by its presence in my life, or without *denying* its presence in my life. After all, so many wonderful gifts have come to me through my recovery.

I AM A DIVINE EXPRESSION OF THE VERY POWER THAT CREATES THE UNIVERSE. I believe in the absolute truth of that statement, so how can I make any "I AM" statements connected to powerlessness? My reality can never include a powerless "I AM" statement. However, it is completely accurate to say that my addicted ego-self is powerless over alcohol, food, and a lot of other things! This is such a freeing philosophy. It gives us permission to be co-creators of the Universe, and it defines who I am in terms of divine power rather than abhorrent behavior. It also allows me to forgive myself and others, for I am able to separate spiritual essence from personality. I never again have to vocalize limiting beliefs, and I can still go to meetings and share my experience, strength, and hope.

We need to allow ourselves time to develop ways of speaking about our addictions that support our beliefs about the world and our place in it. We need to avoid being preachy or smug. After all, the need "to be right" was something many of us brought to the "Addiction 101" class. Walking quietly but purposefully in your Power is the most beneficial way to share your recovery with others.

Another beneficial result of only making positive "I AM" statements is that we release the need to be a victim. Any time that I assume responsibility as opposed to accepting blame, I become powerful and take charge of my own destiny.

The simple act of acknowledging my addicted ego-self along with its need to protect me from pain means that I cannot be a victim. I simply move from that needy space into a position of Power. There is no need to blame ourselves or others for alcoholism or any addiction. I assign responsibility to my addicted ego-self and move on.

Before I was able to move further on in my personal journey, though, I had to sit down, get quiet, and write out as many powerful, positive "I AM" affirmations as I could. I said those affirmations over and over until they became second nature to me. Many of those initial affirmations form what I call my "core affirmations" today.

I still remember how painful and frightening it was for me in recovery to have these empowering Meta-physical-Spiritual beliefs, and to sit in meetings and hear people make statements such as: "I am nuts." "I'll always be sick; I'll never be well." "Without this program, I am nothing." "If I ever leave and go back out there, I will die," and so on.

Of course, none of these things have to be true. You don't have to be nuts. You don't always have to be sick. You don't have to die (not now anyway).

Find a philosophy or spiritual path that supports who you are. If you find that others are discouraging your positive "I AM" statements, then go someplace else where you *are* supported.

The moment you become willing to change is the moment your Higher Self can kick in with unlimited power. So, even though my addicted ego-self wants to eat and drink until the cows come home, I AM A MAN OF POWER; I AM A DIVINE, ETERNAL EXPRESSION OF THE FORCE; I AM HAPPY, WHOLE, AND COMPLETE.

So, let's face facts. If alcohol or fried foods or sugar or marijuana or cocaine or (fill in the blank) worked, we would all have been fixed long ago.

Affirm the Positive

What does work? Accepting your own power and defining for yourself who you want to be! That works, and it works consistently, not just in months with an *R* or in certain rooms!

Stand erect, face the world, and say: "I AM POWER-FUL. I AM WELL." As you sit quietly in meditation, declare your willingness to grow and to be open to your highest good. If the crazy thoughts of your addicted ego-self come into your head, don't fight them! That only engages you in battle. Rather, say firmly to yourself: "I AM WELL." At all costs, you must avoid making negative "I AM" statements.

The question I'm often asked about meetings is: "Well, Robert, if you won't say, 'I am an alcoholic,' what do you say when you're at a meeting?"

Well, one thing I want to avoid, along with negative "I AM" statements, is controversy. Meetings are filled with people successfully undertaking their recovery, but also with scared, hurting folks. I don't want to add to their confusion, so if I'm asked to share (which happens less and less!), I state simply: "My name is Robert, and I AM in recovery from alcoholism." Who can argue with that? It is a statement of fact and an affirmation of power.

My ego-self's addiction is not the theme of my life—a

dramatic influence, most definitely, but not the theme. I have consciously chosen the theme of this lifetime to be spiritual awareness. And, again, it amazes me how Spirit can take all the addiction drama and, like some alchemist from the Middle Ages, transform all those disabilities into spiritual treasures.

What about finding yourself in meetings where all you're hearing are addiction horror tales and precious few recovery stories? Actually, this has happened to me and to many other metaphysically powerful people. Yet, despite those concerns, we still want to be there to share our recovery, our experience, strength, and hope.

There is an appropriate time in the recovery process to share stories of our addicted ego-self's powerlessness over alcohol, and so on. However, after accepting our own Power, these "horror stories" become trite, mundane, and actually boring. I'd much rather talk about my recovery than my ego-self's addiction. Still, it is important for newcomers to hear that those of us who have been recovering for some time now, do remember what it's like to see life through the fog of addiction.

When I go to meetings, I share my recovery as it is now. That is the greatest gift I can possibly give. The proof of the pudding is in the tasting. This Metaphysical Spirituality can be used hand in hand with the Steps as they are now, instead of as an alternative to them. That way we avoid controversy.

Even though working Step One focuses on "powerlessness," this does not imply inaction. In fact, quite the opposite is true. Acknowledging powerlessness is, on one level, an intellectual process, but on other levels, it calls us to action in our outer awareness. I believe we have a moral responsibility to replace what we have come to see as destructive behavior with actions that are supportive of ourselves and the communities of which we find ourselves a part. This creation of alternative behaviors, both the inner awareness and outer awareness, is the foundation upon which responsibility is built.

The Nature of Responsibility

Sometimes people assume that acknowledging addiction powerlessness lets them off the hook as far as responsibility is concerned. This immature assumption is usually just a stage of recovery and is connected to a feeling of great relief. This feeling of relief is important, for all too often the addicted ego-self has blamed all the world's ills upon the addictive process. Now that we begin to see that insanity is a predictable outcome of alcoholism, and so on, we put 2 and 2 together and come up with 4. We can begin to see that most (if not all) of the craziness is due to addiction, rather than due to our being rotten, miserable failures. We can begin to distinguish between (A) the powerlessness of our addicted-ego self's behavior, and (B) the ability of our competent ego-self to assume responsibility for life choices.

Look for just a moment at the word *responsibility*. The root is *response*, so in one sense, it means "being able to respond," and I believe it implies that the response ought to be mature, supportive, and never harmful to ourselves or others. In my work with clients, I have so often seen a little light switch go on behind the eyes when a client "gets it"—that their assuming responsibility is freeing, not restrictive! "Getting it" means that at the very beginning of recovery we know that we have the ability to respond to life from an inner place of power, rather than react from an outer place of automatic addictive reflex. I also see clients breathe a huge sigh of relief when they embrace the freedom of responsibility and release the blame of being an "addict." This, to me, is obvious proof of the power of the words we choose. This simple shift away from "dis-ease" to "em-powerment" opens new galaxies of possibilities for living life creatively.

For those who find themselves working Step One right now, I believe you will find it helpful to make some written notes. First, at the top of a notebook or journal page, write the word *reaction* and at the top of another, write the word *responsibility*. On the page headed "reaction," begin writing down the behaviors, events, and so forth, that reveal the insanity of your addictive process. Remember as you list these "responsibility" and "reaction" behaviors that your addictive process has affected not only yourself, but other people and things in your life. So, as you identify your ability to respond powerfully, and differentiate it from the purely reflexive reactions of your addictive process, note how you would handle things differently today. It's a good idea to keep these notations in a journal for subsequent review. They will also be a valuable resource when you begin sharing your experience, strength, and hope with others.

I predict that you will be surprised by the way in which others will be attracted to the Light of your recovery. You will probably find yourself being asked to be a sponsor far more often than you're able to accept. The inner work you do in Step One will have far-reaching effects—not just on your own recovery alone—but on that of many others, most of whom you probably haven't even met yet. Just as your addictive process harmed others, your recovery will enrich others. You will become especially conscious of this later on as you begin working Step Four.

Continue to remind yourself that working Step One is a process, not an event. In other words, this is not an experience that is finished once and for all. Step One—indeed all of recovery—is a series of ongoing experiences that continue to deepen spirituality, enhance creativity, and urge others toward recovery. For the sake of achieving balance, continue to remind yourself of the positive, supportive aspects of your life, even while you are in the midst of your addictive process. No one or no thing is all good or all bad. Embrace your humanity through acknowledging your divinity.

The Power of Affirmations

I also suggest that as you work Step One, you make time to sit quietly and write out some powerful affirmations. At the end of chapters 1 to 12, you will find some affirmations that I have written, designed to focus attention on the themes of each individual Step. Feel free to use them as they are or to adapt them in any way that supports you.

Some areas you might want to create affirmations about are: your interpersonal relationships; your physical, mental, emotional, and spiritual health; your hobbies or pastimes, and so on. Although your affirmations may be as complex as you wish, I recommend that you keep them simple, and focused on your recovery as it relates to the areas listed above. As your recovery progresses, your affirmations need to keep pace and become reflective of your growing areas of concern.

While you work on compiling your own affirmations, I recommend the work of Stuart Wilde, especially his book, *Affirmations*. Stuart has a humorous, no-nonsense approach that cuts quickly to the chase. I also recommend Louise Hay's inspirational book, *You Can Heal Your Life*, as a rich source from which to mine your own affirmational gems.

To further enhance the affirmation process, find a place where you can sit quietly. Light a candle, play some nice music in the background, and practice writing positive statements about yourself. Notice that the statements need to be about you. Please do not include other people in your affirmations. You may bless others, or you may release others, but refrain from affirming a reality for anyone but yourself.

Your affirmations will almost certainly change as

your recovery progresses. I know that, for myself, the re-education that affirmational work has provided me is the center around which my recovery revolves. For now, I know who and what I truly am. My continuing to differentiate between powerlessness and responsibility while working Step One and consciously opting for responsibility is one of the foundation stones of my recovery. Had I not, with my own eyes, witnessed the cumulative effect of affirmations, I would not insist so strongly upon the essential nature of using them as part of recovery. Just as we release negative, unsupportive beliefs, we must refill that void with supportive "I AM" statements.

Now, while you are redefining your recovery, remember that you can include affirmational work in any area of your life. You are free, even encouraged, to begin visualizing changes that you want to make; yet, resist the impulse to overwhelm yourself. Keep your focus centered on the areas of life most closely connected to your immediate recovery.

SUGGESTED AFFIRMATIONS

You might wish to recite these affirmations on a daily basis while working Step One.

- I AM A DIVINE EXPRESSION OF SPIRIT IN A HUMAN BODY.

- I AM CALM, CENTERED, AND AWARE.

- I NOW OPEN MYSELF TO TRANSFORMING THE POWERLESSNESS OF MY ADDICTED EGO-SELF INTO SPIRITUAL AWARENESS AND UNDERSTANDING.

- I NOW OPEN MYSELF TO THE UNLIMITED POSSIBILITIES OF RECOVERY.

- I NOW RELEASE ANY PERSON, PLACE, OR THING FROM MY LIFE THAT KEEPS THE PERFECT ENJOYMENT OF RECOVERY FROM ME.

- MY RECOVERY AND THE NEW LIFE IT BRINGS ME NOW BECOMES MY PRIORITY.

- ALL IS WELL.

ACTIVITY 1, STEP ONE

In your mind's eye, visualize your addictive process as the trunk of a tree. This tree has roots that spread out all around you. Spend some quiet time thinking about the beginnings of your addictive process.

Now, write down some of the behaviors, traits, beliefs, and so on, that could possibly be connected to the nourishing of your addictive process, just as roots nourish the tree. You could even draw a tree with roots if it helps you visualize more easily. This new awareness can help you embark on alternative ways of relating that will support your recovery.

ACTIVITY 2, STEP ONE

List some patterns or behaviors in your family that might be connected to your addictive process.

A.	E.
B.	F.
C.	G.
D.	H.

Do you feel powerless over any of these patterns or behaviors? Which ones?

A.	E.
B.	F.
C.	G.
D.	H.

Which of these patterns or behaviors do you feel you can change?

A.	E.
B.	F.
C.	G.
D.	H.

Give some thought to how you can change them.

ACTIVITY 3, STEP ONE

Explain how these issues and areas of life are closely connected to your immediate recovery.

A. *Sobriety/Abstinence:*

B. *Spouse/Significant Other:*

C. *Family:*

D. *Career:*

E. *Finances:*

F. *Health:*

G. *Friends:*

H. *Other:*

NOTES ON STEP ONE

Write down any other thoughts, feelings, or revelations associated with Step One.

■ Chapter 2 ■

Step Two: Embracing Hope

**"CAME TO BELIEVE THAT A POWER GREATER
THAN OURSELVES COULD RESTORE US
TO SANITY."**

For those of us walking a path of Metaphysical
Spirituality, belief in Spirit or a Power greater than
our individual personalities is not a difficult concept
to grasp or accept. In fact, it is a concept that we
usually honor each day through our "I AM" affirmations.

The main issue to address in Step Two is the ac-
knowledgement of a Power that can control our addictions. We already know, of course, that alcohol is
more powerful than our addicted ego-selves. But,
alcohol can obviously be controlled by our Higher
Selves (our Divine Essence). After all, there is still alcohol at every turn in this society, yet I AM sober and
in recovery. So alcohol itself cannot be the issue. Addiction, on the level of the addicted ego-self, is the
problem.

When I speak of a "Power greater than myself," I
mean my competent adult ego-self hand in hand with
my Higher Self, so that I need not put my trust in some
nebulous concept outside myself, which I may or may
not connect with. I AM a divine being, so through link-

ing my destiny consciously to a loving, accepting, forgiving Power, I AM assured of recovery. It is not, then, a gift from a power *outside* myself, but rather the natural consequence of connecting to the Knowing *inside* myself.

I remember many misty, muggy New Orleans mornings when my friends and I contemplated life over tall, tropical drinks and platters of grillades and grits in the French Quarter. Of course, we still hadn't gone to bed yet from the last night's party. I had lived life through the direction of my addicted ego-self (immediate gratification, I believe it is called!).

Now, I was not some dreadful sinner in need of redemption. My heart was quite open, yet my vision was clouded by the alcohol addiction of my ego-self. Almost all, if not all, of my affirmations were negative I AM statements. I often cried out to the God of my childhood, but the heavens remained silent. Spirit was speaking in my heart, though, and that is the Power greater than ego! That Inner Knowing, that gentle voice of the heart! That Power greater than any of my ego-selves! That spark of divinity glowing within! It seems so simple now, with years of hindsight, but at the time it was frightening to contemplate giving up alcohol, overeating, and limiting beliefs all at once. Even more daunting, though, was the thought of life as a "sinful" compulsive eater and drunk!

So, in a 12 Step setting, I received the support that I needed to embark on my journey of recovery and discovery. I will always be grateful to those who helped me.

Restoring Health

The root of the English word *sanity* is *sanitas*, the Latin word for health; hence, our use of the word *sanitary* when referring to cleanliness. Being returned to sanity, then, means being restored to health! When we release the expectation that the ego will deliver on its promises and connect with the Power within, we no longer experience dis-ease. Instead, we experience comfort, health, happiness, and connectedness. Service to others becomes a pleasure, where before it was an unpleasant chore that we resented.

It is absolutely essential that we place the addicted ego-self and its insanity in the scrapbook of yesteryear's experience so that we view all that simply as experience that we had on life's journey through the material world. These mementos must never be viewed as our life's theme. As Ram Dass says, it was only "grist for the mill" . . . just stuff.

So when you are working Step Two, keep in mind that your Personal Power is greater than any addictive process. While you are focused on the Higher Power, be very, very careful about your "I AM" statements. Work doubletime with your affirmations. Seek out other metaphysically oriented folks who are 12 Steppers. Hang out with the winners. Declare yourself "in."

Sure, we've all heard these things before. It is nothing new, really. What can be new, though, is manifesting all these things at once. If recovering can be so power-full, why not go for it?

Actually, people can think of hundreds of reasons for not accessing their Personal Power. Most of these reasons for "not going for it" will seem to make perfect sense when viewed from a position of in-sanity. What must be remembered is that there are veils and filters in place that keep a clear perspective at arm's length. These veils and filters are a part of the thought system employed by the addictive process. Some call this crazy thought system "denial," yet denial is only a part of it. There are other components of that system, some of which were actually set up in lifetimes before this one.

While I do believe that it is important to disconnect the wiring of as many of these past-life buttons as possible, Step Two is not necessarily the place to begin that work. It is, though, the perfect place to mention it and to become aware of that fact. Simply, the recognition of how multidimensional the addictive process is will make the necessity of a Power that is much greater than any ego very apparent! This recognition of the connection the addictive process has with past lives and with the challenges of this present lifetime also remove the recovery process from the arena of a "moral failure."

Releasing the Addictive Process

I am continually amazed by how people want to hold on to their "sins" and "moral failures." Why is this so? Well, obviously, the addictive process is pleased to use guilt and shame as excuses to drink or otherwise crank up the insanity. Evident, as well, is the low self-esteem most, if not all, addicts share. Perhaps not so apparent is the reluctance to believe that we really are masters of our own destiny. Releasing the addictive process means letting go of all our excuses. Once we really step out and believe that a Power greater than our ego-selves can restore sanity, we must accept responsibility for what we do with that belief. We need to see that we, ourselves, are responsible for taking some positive action, not waiting for some outside source to come to the rescue. We must keep in mind that THE POWER GREATER THAN OUR (EGO-) SELVES IS OUR HIGHER SELF! The Power that can restore us to sanity is the TRUE SELF, whom we always have been and always will be.

Now, my opinion with respect to working Step Two is that we need to have as much fun as possible with this stage of recovery. Okay, so you will probably notice that I say this about every Step! One of the main points of this book is that we can do serious work and feel a full spectrum of emotions and have fun doing it. Smiles are uplifting. Laughter is healing. So, sit down with pen and paper (or your keyboard), and have fun writing about your restored sanity.

How are things going to be different in recovery? What will your job be like? What relationship changes might be in store? If you are beginning recovery from compulsive eating, can you visualize any changes in your body? Let go and have some fun with this notion. By giving free rein to your imagination, you can dispel some of the negative ego "seriousness" that masquerades as commitment, but which is actually producing criticism and blame. This creative use of imagination is going to bring balance to your recovery.

Keep these written records, and review them from time to time. Watch how your priorities change. Note what has been achieved and what you still want to work on. Observe how your reality is being created and manifested from the inside toward the outside. Your dreams and visions are materialized in your exterior reality only when they have been conceived and nurtured in your thoughts and your heart ON A CONSISTENT BASIS.

Right this moment, at the beginning of your recovery, accept that there will be moments that you will experience as less than what you wanted. Accept, as well, that there are going to be moments of great victory. Which are you going to consciously and consistently give the energy of your belief to?

SUGGESTED AFFIRMATIONS

You might wish to recite these affirmations on a daily basis while working Step Two.

- I BELIEVE THAT MY HIGHER SELF IS A POWER GREATER THAN ANY ADDICTIVE PROCESS.

- I NOW ACCEPT THE GUIDANCE OF MY HIGHER SELF IN MY RECOVERY.

- I DECLARE MY INTENTION OF BEING RESTORED TO SANITY.

- I AM A DIVINE BEING IN PERFECT MENTAL, PHYSICAL, EMOTIONAL, AND SPIRITUAL HEALTH.

- I CONSISTENTLY WALK MY PATH IN BALANCE AND HARMONY.

- ALL IS WELL.

ACTIVITY 1, STEP TWO

List any areas of your life where you feel you could use help or guidance.

A.   E.

B.   F.

C.   G.

D.   H.

Now, list any personal strengths that would allow you to help others.

A.   E.

B.   F.

C.   G.

D.   H.

Finally, examine both of these lists carefully. Now, prioritize the areas needing help and beside each, write one of your strengths that would counteract this limitation. You may also record the names of friends (or even books) that might serve to empower you.

A.   E.

B.   F.

C.   G.

D.   H.

ACTIVITY 2, STEP TWO

List some characteristics that a "Power greater than yourself" would possess. Spend some time thinking about each of these traits and where or in whom you could find them.

A.   F.

B.   G.

C.   H.

D.   I.

E.   J.

Now, explain how you would feel turning control over to that Power.

ACTIVITY 3, STEP TWO

You can raise your self-esteem by releasing judgment. Rather than discuss moral failure, list below some short-term goals for the coming week. Next to each of those short-term goals (which could be "I say my affirmations daily"), write one or two benefits that might result from those simple actions on your part.

SHORT-TERM GOALS: BENEFITS TO MY RECOVERY:

A.   A.

B.   B.

C.   C.

D.   D.

E.   E.

F.   F.

Now, write a few sentences telling how these short-term goals, through enhancing your self-esteem, become the foundation upon which all of your long-term goals for recovery are formulated and achieved. Again, give free "rein and reign" to your creative imagination.

NOTES ON STEP TWO

Write down any other thoughts, feelings, or revelations associated with Step Two.

Chapter 3

Step Three: Turning It Over to Spirit

**"MADE A DECISION TO TURN OUR WILL AND
OUR LIVES OVER TO THE CARE OF GOD AS WE
UNDERSTOOD HIM."**

For those of us walking a path of Metaphysical
Spirituality, the concept of God is usually different
from that of the dominant Judeo-Christian culture. It
is, therefore, essential that we have a concept of God
that is loving, forgiving, and powerful. Personally, I
almost always use the word *Spirit*, with a capital *S*, to
describe my concept of the Force. I tend to avoid the
word *God*, not because I am uncomfortable with it, but
because many people have been severely abused by
religion, and their abusers use *God* to justify that
abuse. So, for now, let's try to use *Spirit* for God and
Higher Self for that spark of divinity inside ourselves.
Later on in the book, you will note my occasional use
of the word *God*. If those mentions make you uncomfortable, find another term and substitute it.

The Role of Spirit

There is really no mystery about what Spirit's will
is for us. Spirit wills that we be happy.

Ego wills that it always be right, always get its way,

that others are wrong, that it alone knows what is best. Now, it's not that ego is "bad"; it is just limited. Spirit is unlimited. Ego offers us five dollars an hour; Spirit makes us full partners in a multimillion dollar corporation. Still, there are some who continue to choose the lower rate. I can't explain that, but today I choose union with my Higher Self and Spirit's destiny.

If you attend meetings regularly, you will soon discover that even though Step Three says: "God as we understood Him," there is pressure to conform to the established Judeo-Christian concept of God. Sometimes this pressure is subtle, sometimes, quite blatant. There are certain parts of the country so dominated by Fundamentalist Christianity that 12 Step meetings are often indistinguishable from Wednesday night prayer meetings. Well, at least the participants aren't drinking.

But what about our Metaphysical Spirituality? I remain convinced that we can still attend meetings and seek out each other for support. We need to avoid controversy. We do not need a battle.

So, right now, let's get quiet and say, "I surrender my ego to the direction and control of my Higher Self and Spirit." I hope, too, that it is immediately evident that I do not assign any gender to the Creative Force of the Universe. Spirit is an "It," quite beyond the time-space limitations of an incarnation in the material world. We experience Spirit multidimensionally. I mean by this that we touch Spirit with our hearts, but also with our ego experiences. Therefore, it doesn't have to be scary to turn our ego power over to our Higher Self and Spirit.

When I was a child, I was taught that God was a father figure who got upset and offended very easily. Usually, you didn't have any idea you'd offended this God until it was too late! Now, I realize that this was a case of humankind creating a God in the image of its own limitations. Metaphysical newcomers to 12 Step programs certainly don't want to turn their will and lives over to such a fickle, angry deity with such a penchant for vengeance. After all, most of us have made mistakes in recovery. So, whether you are a traditional follower of Judeo-Christian beliefs or a student of Metaphysical Spirituality, take some time to think about the concept of Spirit without any limitations. I suspect, sometimes, that many people don't move far beyond third-grade catechism or Sunday School in their concept of Spirit. This, naturally, would limit the progress that they can make with Step Three.

So, again, be patient with yourself and others. Give your Higher Self and Spirit some room to work for your Highest Good. Avoid preaching at others or yourself. In meetings, share your experience, strength, and hope. Then, be quiet and listen.

What Spirit Knows

Spirit, as I understand it, wills that I know that: I AM POWERFUL; I AM WORTHY AND DESERVING OF ALL THE ABUNDANCE OF THE UNIVERSE; I AM LOVABLE; I AM SAFE IN A WORLD THAT SUP-

YOUR COMPANION TO 12 STEP RECOVERY

PORTS ME; I ENJOY SHARING MY RECOVERY
WITH OTHERS; I LOVE AND BLESS MY VARIOUS
EGO-SELVES AND JOYFULLY ACCEPT THE GIFTS
THEY BRING ME; MY HIGHER SELF NOW DI-
RECTS MY LIFE; I EXPERIENCE LIFE AS POSI-
TIVE, SUPPORTIVE, AND EXCITING.

I also know that Spirit does not intend for me to
suffer any lack or imbalance. There is nothing to be
punished for or to answer for. There is only ego confusion for Spirit to balance out. The very act of deciding to relinquish ego control to my Higher Self frees
me. This is what I have always considered so beautiful about Step Three, for it is not when we turn our ego
control over to Spirit that we work the Step; it is when
we "decide" to turn over ego control to Spirit that we
become free! So, it is not some action we take in our
outer world, but rather a shift that occurs within. It
is empowering to discover that recovery begins in the
individual as a resonance inside the heart and not as
a "decision" in the intellect. After all, oldtimers remind us often that our best reasoning led us to be addicts in the first place.

For we metaphysically oriented people to say, "Not
my will, but thine," we mean, "Not the rambling dialogue of my addicted ego-self, but the centered Wisdom of my Higher Self and Spirit." Remember, this
is not a put-down of our ego personalities or of any of
our experiences in the material world. It's a prioritiz-
ing of values while bringing these various components
of personality into balance and harmony.

So often, the very things we curse in life turn out to

be great gifts. Alcoholism and compulsive eating have taught me a compassion and wisdom I could never have come by any other way. Of course, I see this now, well into recovery. It certainly was not that apparent in the midst of all my pain.

The Reality of Step Three

Step Three works with Metaphysical Spirituality as effectively as it does with any other spirituality. The difference is in the particulars of the way in which we approach Spirit.

I have often had clients and sponsorees complain that I expected too much of them in Step Three. When I questioned them, we inevitably discovered that they were expecting too much of themselves, too quickly. They were looking at my years of recovery well into its own process, assuming that I expected the same of them RIGHT NOW! It was a great lesson for me in the beginning of my work with clients to be reminded of the nature of my own recovery—to realize anew that my recovery is a dwelling built brick by brick, one at a time. When newcomers look at our dwellings, it is natural for them to feel overwhelmed. It needs to become natural for you, as you progress in your own recovery, to remind newcomers (and clients) of the cumulative nature of recovery. Remember, we call it the 12 STEPS, not the 12 EVENTS!

12 Step recovery has the great potential of transforming us from harsh judgment into gentle acceptance (live and let live). Again, we need to keep in mind

that very often we were taught that God is harsh and judgmental. Then, naturally, wanting to be like God, we became harshly judgmental ourselves. Does it not make sense that we will imitate what is held out to us by our mentors (parents, teachers, ministers, etc.)? So, there is no need to blame them or ourselves, or God. They were teaching us what they had been taught about God. Then, to compound the issue, there came to be all kinds of cultural, racial, sexual, and tribal components layered around what we were taught about God. We came to see that in order to discover for ourselves what God means to us, we had to re-assess much of the culture and its validity in our lives.

As I wrote earlier, some of us began to see that we had created God in our own image! Every human foible had been ascribed to God. God became a "He." God became jealous. God became vindictive. God became capable of erratic, unpredictable behavior. God became punishing or rewarding, depending upon whom you asked.

Of course, all the attributes listed above are quite human, not divine. But, many of us still acted as if the problem were with God rather than with our concepts about God. Naturally, we brought all this baggage into our addictive process, and these crazy ideas about God provided much of the fear and guilt that fueled our addictive insanity. Many of us actually became addicted to religion! Now, there's a cosmic twist.

There have been times when a client or a sponsoree would assume that I expected them, in Step Three, to release all the insanity and come up with supportive, mature concepts of God by noon, next Wednesday. Of course, that is not the case. Step Three is where the process of a personalized "understanding" of God BE-GINS. I know that, for myself, this process of a personal "understanding" of God continues, and I expect it to be an ongoing component of my recovery and my Walk with Spirit this time around.

It can be seen as overwhelming only if you expect this step to be an "event" instead of a process. Take your time. Have fun understanding God. Let God teach you about the cosmic sense of humor that permeates all of Creation. Believe me, when you begin looking at things in this way, you'll laugh a lot.

Now, no one is qualified to dictate how you begin to "understand" God. It is a step so intensely personal that I hesitate to write about it. Yet, because of its intensely personal nature, I feel compelled to write about it! Therefore, I suggest you begin this process with pen and paper.

Find a place where you can sit quietly and think. Write down any quality or attribute of God that you can think of. Be honest. Even if you are afraid of being "punished," go ahead and courageously list what you've been taught about God.

When you've spent some time writing about your past understanding of God, write down the qualities and attributes that you think God needs to have right now in order to be a positive presence in your recovery. What thoughts about God do you need to release? Write them down! What ideas about God do you need to adopt and incorporate into your new life of recovery? Please, write those down! Again, allow me to remind you to keep these writings and review them often, for surely, as you grow, so will your "understanding" of God grow. It is a process, not an event.

Now, if you're already tired of hearing me say, "It is a process, not an event," remember that this idea frees us to experience the multidimensionality of recovery without the linear concept of "beginning and end"-type events. We have eternity, one day at a time.

If you are one of the fortunate few who were taught positive, supportive concepts of God, accept my congratulations and move on to Step Four. All the rest of us need to continue keeping a God-journal where we can watch ourselves grow along with our "understanding" of God. We can also begin seeing and appreciating how the reality of our recovery proceeds from the inner awareness through to the outer awareness. This is important to realize, for many of us have a history of putting the cart before the horse. We have assumed that our lives would be perfectly happy when we stopped drinking, smoking, under/over eating, abusing drugs, and so on. We now know that it is just the opposite. We need to remind ourselves on a daily basis that it is far more important to BE spiritual than to LOOK spiritual. It is far more fun to BE successful than to LOOK successful. This concept will become clearer as you work Step Four to a greater extent. It will also assist in the taking of a more accurate and thorough inventory in this Step, when the basis for taking this inventory is a loving, supportive "understanding" of God.

SUGGESTED AFFIRMATIONS

You might wish to recite these affirmations on a daily basis while working Step Three.

- ALL MY THOUGHTS AND IDEAS ABOUT GOD ARE LOVING AND SUPPORTIVE OF RECOVERY.

- TODAY, I CONSCIOUSLY OPEN MYSELF TO MY SUPPORTIVE UNDERSTANDING OF GOD.

- GOD'S WILL FOR ME IS THAT I BE HAPPY.

- I TURN OVER MY EGO-WILL TO THE CARE AND DIRECTION OF MY HIGHER SELF.

- I JOYFULLY SHARE MY RECOVERY WITH OTHERS.

- ALL IS WELL.

ACTIVITY 1, STEP THREE

UNDERSTANDING GOD

I. List some of the unsupportive beliefs about God that have hindered you in the past.

    A.

    B.

    C.

    D.

    E.

    F.

    G.

    H.

    I.

II. Now list some new, supportive ideas about God that will aid you in your personal growth.

    A.

    B.

    C.

    D.

    E.

    F.

    G.

    H.

    I.

ACTIVITY 2, STEP THREE

This activity will allow you to use the creative power of your imagination. Share this activity with a close friend if you wish. Relax and have fun with it.

Imagine that your addictive process could be magically removed right now. Explain how your life would be different.

Now, with our magic wand in hand once again, visualize what your life would be like today if you'd never had addiction in your life. Write down your thoughts.

ACTIVITY 3, STEP THREE

Examine the previous activity closely. Are there any things you would trust Spirit to take charge of right now. What are they?

A.   E.

B.   F.

C.   G.

D.   H.

Explain why you feel the way you do.

NOTES ON STEP THREE

Write down any other thoughts, feelings, or revelations associated with Step Three.

Chapter 4

Step Four: Striving for Balance

"MADE A SEARCHING AND FEARLESS MORAL INVENTORY OF OURSELVES."

Working Step Four can be an area where the self-empowerment and self-illumination of our Metaphysical Spirituality is made evident in a dramatic way. This is where we can consciously release the need to blame ourselves or others and accept personal responsibility! I cannot conceive of any action that could be more freeing at this stage of recovery.

So much of the addictive process involves us blaming ourselves or others for our troubles. Naturally, when we assign blame, whether to ourselves or to others, we lay on guilt in addition to the blame. And, when someone is guilty . . . they have to pay! This cycle of blame, guilt, and revenge provides fuel for the fire of alcoholism, compulsive eating, drugs, and so on. Is it any wonder that it is such a challenge communicating with someone in the midst of their addiction?

Sometimes, well-meaning people use Step Four as another excuse to beat themselves up. They make long lists of every fault, minor or major, that they can think of. They use these dirty-laundry lists as further proof of their unworthiness. This concept is utterly foreign to those of us who walk a path of Metaphysical Power and Spirituality today.

There was a time when these dirty-laundry lists seamed quite normal, though. When I was younger, before I really discovered the power of words and thoughts, I spent hours "examining my conscience" before going into confession. Nothing was too trivial to mention, though I did fudge a bit on some of the biggies! So, I certainly do understand the tendency of the addicted ego-self to concentrate on what is "wrong."

If you are to work Step Four from a position of your personal power and Metaphysical Spirituality, one thing to do is this: Write out your successes along with the things you regret or wish to change. You need to celebrate the areas of your life that have remained un-scarred by your addiction. Making your inventory with the help and direction of your Higher Self can be one of the most powerful experiences of your recovery process.

Declare Your Intentions

Light some incense and candles, put on some soft music, get a favorite crystal, stone, or other power object, and forcefully declare your intention aloud, a very important act before undertaking any spiritual venture. Your declaration could go something like this:

I DECLARE THAT I AM A SERVANT OF LIGHT. I CLAIM THIS MOMENT OF POWER. I NOW LIST ALL

MY ASSETS AND ALL THE DEBTS OF MY EGO-
PERSONALITY. I NOW WORK STEP FOUR FOR
MY HIGHEST GOOD. I RELEASE THE NEED TO
BLAME. I ACCEPT PERSONAL RESPONSIBILITY
FOR ALL MY ACTIONS AND CIRCUMSTANCES. I
NOW FORGIVE MYSELF AND ALL WHO NEED
FORGIVING. I NOW RELEASE ANY CLAIM TO
REVENGE. AS A SPARK OF THE POWER THAT
CREATES THE UNIVERSE, I NOW DECLARE MY-
SELF TO BE IN PERFECT PHYSICAL, MEN-
TAL, EMOTIONAL, AND SPIRITUAL HEALTH. ALL
IS WELL.

When you have made your declaration of intention,
examine the past and the present in terms of your Personal Power as well as in terms of your addicted ego-
self. For example, if you list "I used the rent money
to buy beer," then balance that with "I pulled a drown-
ing child from a raging river torrent." Or, if you
haven't saved a child from a watery grave, then find
something equally as marvelous that you have done.
The point is balance and harmony. Also, I encourage
you to have fun with this process. Pretend that you
have some of the guys from Monty Python there along
with you and your sponsor! Imagine that John Cleese
is the Minister of Silly Walks, helping you to evaluate
the ego-addictive process. In this way, you can diffuse
some of the psychic intensity surrounding your addiction.

Of course, all this is not to say that we're not being

serious. We are certainly serious and committed to recovery. However, laughter is far more healing than sourpuss blaming.

Another important point to consider when working your Fourth Step is this: You are only responsible for making an inventory of YOUR life (this present lifetime, please . . . there will be plenty of time for past lives, later!). Avoid the temptation to inventory your spouse, your partner, best friend, parents, the President, or the mean old man down the block who sprayed you and your dog with his garden hose.

In the Fourth Step, we search ourselves, not the world. Metaphysically, Step Four allows us to accept responsibility for our mistakes and accept credit for our successes. The Metaphysical-Spiritual path involves the continual search for balance and harmony.

When I work with clients or with program members, I am always amazed by their willingness to discuss mistakes and their reluctance to discuss successes. I ask them to read or reread *You Can Heal Your Life*, by Louise Hay, and I remind them of one of my favorite Louise Hay affirmations: "I AM ALLOWED TO MAKE MISTAKES WHILE I AM LEARNING." This one powerful affirmation frees us to experience our divinity and our humanity simultaneously. Our mistakes become the shiny, decorative paper in which the gifts of our spiritual learning are wrapped. If we were to allow fear, shame, or guilt to keep us from our inventory, we might very well miss the reason we chose birth on this planet, in this particular lifetime. The point is not to deny one's humanity, but to embrace it, merging that ego knowing with Higher Self Knowing.

If making this personal inventory is scary, be patient with yourself. Make sure that you find a Metaphysically Spiritual ally (your sponsor) to stand beside you as you undertake this journey.

When I was a child, the seeds of my addiction were planted in my addicted ego-self. No matter what I did, or how well I did it, my parents hit me and yelled at me. On a daily basis, I heard what a disappointment I was to them. The emotional abuse they inflicted on me as a child was far more severe, and certainly more long-lasting, though, than the physical bruises. So, I understand why some people are reluctant to delve into the past.

Yet today, I AM A MAN OF POWER. I EXPERIENCE LIFE AS A COMPETENT ADULT. I share some of the pain of my past with you, not so that I can whine and say, "Oh, poor me," but to share the Knowing that came to me cloaked in pain. My wounds have helped make me a compassionate healer. My emotional hurt and the terror I felt as a child have taught me the real meaning of power and authority. I no longer allow myself to be abused. I never remain silent if others are being abused. When I was a child, there was nothing I could do to defend myself. Today, as a man of Power, I defend not only myself, but I am an advocate for those vulnerable to the abuse of authority. This position of Personal Power came to me as one of the benefits of Step Four, because today I accept responsibility for myself and all my actions.

Before we leave Step Four, I want to write a few things about the word *fearless*. If I suggest that you make a fearless personal inventory, I do not mean that you aren't allowed to feel fear. Feeling afraid can sometimes be a sign of consciousness! What I mean by "fearless" from the perspective of my Metaphysical Spirituality is that I do not allow my fear to paralyze me. I move forward despite fear, alongside fear. I make friends with my fear. I know, today, that the fear was put there originally to protect me. The fear is a part of my personal history in this lifetime, usually connected to my inner child ego-self, addicted ego-self, or adolescent ego-self. Fear can never be a part of my Spiritual Essence, for it can only be expressed through ego personality. And, even then, it can never be negative, if we accept the gifts it brings us.

Working Step Four can be a wonderfully exciting adventure, so relax and be gentle and patient with yourself.

Let Others Help You

Now that you have had some practice writing down "assets" and "debts" in your inventory, I suggest that you find someone who has been in recovery for a while to bounce some ideas off of. This person could be your sponsor or some other friend with a 12 Step background. This person may or may not be the one with whom you choose to share your inventory in Step Five, so remember that in Step Four you might need to protect your privacy (and the privacy of others) by using some discretion.

When you have chosen someone to help you compile your inventory, schedule a time when you can meet together to work on it. You can use the ideas in this book to guide you as well. The point is to make the time you work on your inventory special. Avoid meeting in public. Avoid places in your home where your privacy cannot be assured. Making it special is a sign of the new concern and care you have for yourself.

Remember when you were practicing writing your inventory with the Monty Python gang earlier in this chapter? Well, you need to maintain your ability to laugh now, for some of the things you and your sponsor come up with may make you cry. That, of course, is part of the experience, and is indicative of balance. Our external world is a place where we experience contrast: hot-cold, up-down, yes-no. So, it is perfectly normal to laugh at absurdity and cry due to tragedy, and Step Four is the place to begin this process.

Again, please remember to take your time here. If your sponsor or friend is pushing you too fast, speak up! Practice being assertive without being cruel or obnoxious. Just say something such as, "I need to slow down for a while." There is plenty of time; for, in essence, you will be taking inventory for the rest of your recovery (see Step Ten).

There is no way you can do your inventory "wrong," for it is yours and yours alone. "Right" and "wrong" are not part of the picture. Continue reminding yourself and your sponsor that taking inventory never stops. The way you work on inventory now will surely be different from the way you'll do it as your recovery grows and progresses. In my own life of recovery, it has been a great relief to be able to explore my growth process without worrying about being "wrong," which was previously one of the major joys of my addicted ego-self.

When I discovered my addicted ego-self's inclination toward being "wrong," I asked myself what the payoff was. What did the addicted ego-self have to gain by being "wrong" or by having someone else be "wrong"? There is always a payoff or reward for any ego-self behavior. Personally, the payoff was DRAMA! Almost everything on my "debt" sheet was connected to my ego-self's need for dramatic distraction. Those "debts" were also major excuses for drinking, eating, and otherwise indulging in my addictive process.

Hear this well: THE LOVE OF DRAMA IS THE ROOT OF ALL EVIL! The incessant, insatiable desire of the addicted ego-self for constant diversion and entertainment creates guilt and fear. The resulting drama serves to always keep focus on the outside, never looking inward.

Today, I consciously work on releasing drama as soon as it pops up. I prefer a quiet life: no more bars or clubs, no more all-you-can-eat buffets, no more gossip sessions. (Okay, so not as many gossip sessions as before!) The point of all this talk about drama is to reinforce how useless it is to label ourselves or others as "wrong." Yes, we've made mistakes. Yes, we'll make mistakes again. This is a part of being human. The experience of mistakes and successes is a part of incarnating in the material world.

It's when we begin connecting our love for drama with our addictive process that we, yet again, prove that our insanity is projected from within. However, our recovery is also projected from within.

Make your inventory gently and in peace.

SUGGESTED AFFIRMATIONS

You might wish to recite these affirmations on a daily basis while working Step Four.

- I AM A (WO)MAN OF POWER.

- I ACCEPT MYSELF THE WAY I AM EVEN AS I COMMIT MYSELF TO GROWTH AND CHANGE.

- EVERY PERSON, PLACE, AND THING IN MY LIFE BRINGS GIFTS FOR MY GROWTH.

- I RELEASE ANY BEHAVIOR THAT KEEPS MY RECOVERY AND THE ENJOYMENT OF MY RECOVERY FROM ME.

- TODAY I INTEGRATE THE VARIOUS ASPECTS OF MY PERSONALITY AND EXPRESS MY POWER THROUGH MY COMPETENT EGO-SELF.

- I FEARLESSLY EMBRACE LIFE'S CHALLENGES AS I JOYFULLY SHARE MY RECOVERY.

- I REALLY LOVE MYSELF.

- ALL IS WELL.

ACTIVITY 1, STEP FOUR

List some of your supportive traits and some of your unsupportive traits.

SUPPORTIVE TRAITS: UNSUPPORTIVE TRAITS:

A.   A.

B.   B.

C.   C.

D.   D.

E.   E.

F.   F.

G.   G.

Explain how they are supportive or unsupportive.

Please allow yourself several weeks to work on this activity. After you've spent some time with it, begin Activity 2, Step Four. These two activities will provide you with a wonderfully powerful foundation for taking inventory throughout your recovery.

ACTIVITY 2, STEP FOUR

Visualize times in your life when you felt successful. Dissect that experience inside your imagination. What elements were present in your success?

A.   E.

B.   F.

C.   G.

D.   H.

Now, can you imagine yourself taking these elements and using them to transform unsupportive traits into supportive ones? Explain how.

ACTIVITY 3, STEP FOUR

Write down three things that you fear at this moment, and tell why you fear these things. Next, use your creative imagination to see yourself free of fear's paralyzing grip. Write down what it feels like, right now, to proceed with recovery despite your fear. Susan Jeffers' book, *Feel the Fear and Do It Anyway*, is an inspiring source of self-empowerment at this particular state of recovery.

1. I fear _____ because:

   Being free of fear's grip feels like:

2. I fear _____ because:

   Being free of fear's grip feels like:

3. I fear _____ because:

   Being free of fear's grip feels like:

NOTES ON STEP FOUR

Write down any other thoughts, feelings, or revelations associated with Step Four.

- **Chapter 5** -

Step Five: Speaking the Truth

**"ADMITTED TO GOD, TO OURSELVES, AND TO
ANOTHER HUMAN BEING THE EXACT NATURE
OF OUR WRONGS."**

Here in Step Five, we give our denial process a good
going over! We refuse to let our addicted ego-self keep
secrets. Through working Step Five, we so diffuse the
addicted ego-self that it can no longer blackmail us by
whispering things such as: "If they only knew what
you're really like . . ." or "Suppose they found out
what you've done." The act of speaking aloud empowers the Higher Self as it deflates the frantic pos-
turing of the addicted ego-self.

Remember that the guys and gals who developed the
Steps years ago were coming out of a Judeo-Christian
culture heavy on guilt. So, discovering "wrong" was
very important in their hierarchy of values. God was
up in the sky keeping records of our transgressions.
All in all, I find it to be a negative, limiting concept of
divinity and certainly a depressing view of our place
in the Universe. Trying to please others fueled my addiction, and I certainly learned as a child that I was a
mortal sinner in need of redemption, always being told
how "wrong" I was.

For those of us who have been wounded by traditional religion, Metaphysical Spirituality is a wonderfully empowering alternative. We can work Step Five more fully and more for our highest good by substituting *mistakes* for the word *wrongs*. *Wrong* always implies blame, while *mistake* gives us room to try again, to move on.

Connecting with the Higher Self

From the perspective of my Metaphysical Spirituality, in working Step Five, I connect with my Higher Self in meditation. Experiencing my own divinity allows me to "admit to myself" my humanity. Now, I know that being human, or being in a body, is the vehicle I have chosen on this planet. It is not a "bad" thing. My sisters and brothers also know what it is like being in a human body. We all experience great ecstasy of Spirit in conjunction with the mistakes that we repeatedly make. So, when we choose to evaluate life as this interconnected relationship between our Higher Self, our ego-selves, and all Creation, what is the big deal about mistakes? They allow us to grow!

When you fully work Step Five, you destroy the addicted ego-self's belief system. We usually call this belief system "denial." How can denial operate in your life when you've shined Light on its falsehoods? The bonds of denial can no longer bind us once we speak Truth. And, if something as simple as vocalizing our mistakes accomplishes this goal so quickly and easily, why not go for it?

Working Step Five does not mean that we'll never do

anything stupid again. It only means that our mistakes won't fool us as easily or for as long as they once did.

I suggest that when you acknowledge mistakes to your Higher Self, Spirit, and to another human, that you also acknowledge your strengths. To concentrate only on mistakes will create an imbalance. In Metaphysical Spirituality, we always seek balance and harmony. (Now, how many times have you heard me say that?)

If the person you've chosen to share Step Five with does not agree with or understand this concept, then by all means find someone who does. There is no rigid timetable to follow when doing this delicate work of the heart, so be gentle with yourself. Recovery is a process, not an event. We have the rest of our lives to work on all the ego stuff.

We have come to a point, once again, where it can be beneficial to keep a journal. If you don't like journals or journaling, keep a folder or notebook for writing down the "exact nature" of your assets and debts. How you choose to do this is up to you and your personal preferences. What is important is being able to see in black and white the progression from your initial inventory work onward through your recovery. I also suggest that you date these inventory pages to make viewing your progress easier.

Shining Light on Secrets

It is one thing in Step Four to list assets and debts, but another thing entirely to speak these thoughts aloud to someone else in Step Five. When we do shine Light on secrets, we break the backbone of the denial system. Secrets are seldom health inducing. Secrets that protect safety and privacy are other issues. However, generally speaking, secrets do not support our recovery.

How are secrets unsupportive? Well, as mentioned earlier, guilt and fear are magnets for drama. Drama is a magnet for addictive behavior. Guilt and fear mate together and breed insanity. Even though the addicted ego-self's ability to understand is limited, it does have enough sophistication to realize that telling the truth spells the end of its reign of terror.

Keep in mind, though, that this "reign of terror" has a certain predictable logic to it—the denial system. Our major method of diffusing the denial system is to "Speak Our Truth." This is elaborated upon in Chapter 14, "Odds and Ends."

I believe that assets are as much a part of truth as debts are. I have never been able to understand why Step Five has, from the beginning of the program, omitted mentioning "the exact nature of our rights." It seems so obviously unbalanced to concentrate on "wrongs" alone. Why does this seem so difficult for us to do?

Well, I keep insisting that it is vital for us to achieve balance when taking inventory, because how else can we tell the truth? My "faults," my "wrongs," my "shortcomings," are certainly the truth, but only part of the truth! How can I remain in recovery when I won't acknowledge my assets or my strengths? The answer is, I can't. Therefore, it becomes clear that we HAVE TO EXPAND Step Five in order to tell the truth.

Sometimes people say to me, "But, Robert, if I talk about my good points, people will think I'm conceited. They might accuse me of being stuck-up. Besides, why can't you just work the Steps like everyone else always has?" See? It's clear that if you decide to step out of the crowd, people *will* notice! You'll make yourself a target for the insecurities of others.

When clients or program members ask me those types of questions, I question their self-esteem. I ask about any abuse in their childhood or adolescence. I ask about their experiences with romantic relationships. Can you guess what I almost always discover? A good number of us have suffered from low self-esteem due to childhood abuse, adolescent insecurities, and/or romantic disasters. A good number of all of us are working with affirmations and redefining who we are. We're almost all working a program and/or in therapy.

What in the world would make us afraid of becoming conceited or stuck-up anyway? Most of us have a long way to go in the self-love and self-esteem department before we need to worry about conceit!

Nevertheless, I believe that acknowledging our assets is worth running the risk of being thought of as "stuck-up." Don't you agree? So, when you have completed Step Five to the point of being ready to speak it aloud, when you have chosen a sponsor or friend to share Step Five with as you did in Step Four, find a nice, private, quiet, safe place where you can be with your Higher Self and sponsor and speak your whole Truth. Speaking only part of the truth is risky and dangerous to recovery.

The Truth really does set us free.

SUGGESTED AFFIRMATIONS

You might wish to recite these affirmations on a daily basis while working Step Five.

- I AM A DIVINE EXPRESSION OF SPIRIT IN A HUMAN BODY.

- TODAY, I ACKNOWLEDGE AND EMBRACE MY HUMANITY.

- TODAY, I ALLOW MYSELF TO MAKE MISTAKES WHILE I LEARN.

- I GRATEFULLY ACKNOWLEDGE MY STRENGTHS AND MY WEAKNESSES.

- I NOW TRANSFORM ALL MY FAULTS, THROUGH KNOWLEDGE, INTO ASSETS THAT ENRICH MY RECOVERY.

- TODAY, I ADMIT TO SPIRIT, TO MYSELF, AND TO ALL HUMAN BEINGS MY EXACT NATURE: A DIVINE BEING.

- I GENTLY MOVE FORWARD IN RECOVERY.

- I LOVINGLY RECORD MY PROGRESS AND SHARE MY RECOVERY WITH OTHERS.

- ALL IS WELL.

ACTIVITY 1, STEP FIVE

Use this space to record as many of the characteristics of your denial system as you can. Continue to review this list, and add to it as you see fit. Saying this list aloud greatly decreases its power over you. Refer to the section on "denial" in chapter 14 for further guidance.

BELIEFS THAT FORM MY DENIAL PROCESS:

A.	H.
B.	I.
C.	J.
D.	K.
E.	L.
F.	M.
G.	N.

Explain how you can reprogram these beliefs into supportive Truth.

ACTIVITY 2, STEP FIVE

Review the characteristics listed in your denial system (Activity 1, Step Five). Practice telling yourself the truth about them by writing a positive, supportive affirmation to counter each denial belief. For example, if in Activity 1 you listed "I am fat; therefore, no one loves me," then you could write "I am lovable and supported by all in my life; I am at my healthy, ideal body weight."

A. DENIAL BELIEF:

    MY RECOVERY TRUTH:

B. DENIAL BELIEF:

    MY RECOVERY TRUTH:

C. DENIAL BELIEF:

    MY RECOVERY TRUTH:

D. DENIAL BELIEF:

    MY RECOVERY TRUTH:

ACTIVITY 3, STEP FIVE

Take a few minutes to sit quietly and think of several "mistakes" you've made or times you labeled yourself as "wrong." Now, in light of the spiritual work you've done so far in recovery, list several gifts (for example, insight, compassion, life experience) that come to you now from each "mistake" or "wrong." Isn't it fun to delve beneath the surface and peek at Spirit working in our lives?

MISTAKES:	GIFTS FROM MY MISTAKES:
A.	A.
B.	B.
C.	C.
D.	D.
E.	E.
F.	F.

TIMES I WAS "WRONG":	GIFTS THAT CAME TO ME THROUGH MY "WRONGS":
A.	A.
B.	B.
C.	C.
D.	D.
E.	E.
F.	F.

NOTES ON STEP FIVE

Write down any other thoughts, feelings, or revelations associated with Step Five.

Chapter 6

Step Six: Looking Only Forward

"WERE ENTIRELY READY TO HAVE GOD REMOVE ALL THESE DEFECTS OF CHARACTER."

Well now, really! Who in the world would want to hold on to "defects of character"? Our addicted ego-self, that's who!

However, before we get into the workings of Step Six, I need to mention a basic Metaphysical-Spiritual principle: We never "get rid of" or "remove" things. Once something has come into our lives, it becomes part of our karmic history. Instead, we allow Spirit, along with the Higher Self, to transform limitation into spiritual awareness.

Rather than focus on the "character defects" of our ego, we learn and grow from those patterns, and they actually become the foundation of recovery. When we approach Step Six in this way, we become the agents of change. The multidimensional Higher Self quickens the dense energies of the ego and physical body and actually transmutes those frequencies into dynamic, smoothly flowing consciousness.

Can you see how very different this concept is from the traditional religious teachings embodied in this culture? God is off in the heavens, and we are requesting God to do something to us. We remain these passive, somewhat wimpy, pitiful creatures at the mercy of a God who may or may not respond. Who needs that?

When we become willing to move into a place of Personal Power and responsibility, we become co-creators of recovery along with Spirit. We're not asking any power outside of ourselves to fix us. After all, didn't we become addicts in the first place by expecting something outside of us to come into our lives and make things okay?

At first look, Step Six may seem overly simple. But actually, it is a crucial point to reach in recovery. After you've seen Spirit take these ego weaknesses and transform them into wisdom, compassion, healing, and teaching, it is almost impossible to return to old behavior. If you're driving around in a Porsche, are you likely to exchange it for an ox-cart? Probably not. So, once Spirit transforms ego weakness, that tends to be the pattern we'll seek out from then on. We become magnetized to recovery experiences.

The implication is not that once this transforming weakness into strength takes place, that it is over and done with. Oh, no. We still deal with ego weaknesses. We just go deeper into those issues and touch and transform them in ways we couldn't even imagine possible before.

One of the questions I ask clients or sponsorees is this: "How do you know when you are ENTIRELY ready to have your Higher Self transform your unsupportive traits into positive assets?" Usually, silence is the reply to my question. I sit for a moment and observe how comfortable these people are with silence, and when they start squirming a little, I let them off the hook. It really is a trick question but, nonetheless, an important one to ask.

Were the Step not phrased this way, I don't believe I would ever think in terms of being "entirely ready." After all, I see great progress in simply being "sort of ready" or, even better, just "ready." This is really what the Step implies, I believe.

Being "entirely ready" means that we want to transform all behavior that fails to support us. We do not wish to keep just one or two little foibles, but to be as committed to authentic recovery as possible. There will be no crossing my fingers here. That is what "entirely ready" means.

The reason I mention this point is that we need to be aware that the language of the Steps and the Big Book is a part of a specific decade (the 1920s) and a specific group (fundamentalist religion). I suspect that in 60 or 70 years, the language used in this book will look old-fashioned and perhaps even be confusing due to changing definitions and the passage of time.

As the Step is currently written, I believe it can easily be interpreted in an unbalanced way. The word *defect* implies disability, while the term *defect of character* implies sin or wrongdoing or moral weakness. Of course, there was a time when alcoholism itself was viewed as a "defect of character." I think most people would agree that once we released the perception of alcoholism as a "defect of character," great strides were made in the treatment of addiction. Could it possibly be time now to begin releasing these outdated concepts from the Steps? If so, it begins with you and your willingness to step apart from the acceptability of the crowd. However, you don't have to overwhelm yourself by doing all this right now. Just think about it.

SUGGESTED AFFIRMATIONS

You might wish to recite these affirmations on a daily basis while working Step Six.

- I AM A (WO)MAN OF POWER.

- I ENJOY MY RECOVERY.

- I NOW TRANSFORM ALL EGO LIMITATION INTO STRENGTH, KNOWLEDGE, AND SPIRITUAL POWER.

- MY TRUE NATURE IS MY DIVINE ESSENCE.

- ALL MISTAKES OF MY PAST ARE NOW TRANSFORMED INTO RECOVERY STRENGTHS THAT ENRICH ME AND ALL WHO ARE TOUCHED BY MY LIFE.

- MY RECOVERY MAGNETIZES HEALTH, WEALTH, AND HAPPINESS TO ME.

- MY LANGUAGE NOW REFLECTS MY NEW UNDERSTANDING IN RECOVERY.

- ALL IS WELL.

ACTIVITY 1, STEP SIX

What are some of your ideas about illness? How do these ideas affect your personal addictive process? Use a narrative format for this activity, but also keep a running list of any recurring traits or characteristics that you notice.

RECURRING CHARACTERISTICS:

A.   D.

B.   E.

C.   F.

ACTIVITY 2, STEP SIX

This is another activity that flows well in a narrative form. Spend some time thinking about the difference between the concept of "removing defects of character" and the spiritual concept of "transforming pain into character strength." For example, explain how you could transform "selfishness" into "compassion." Use your powers of imagination and creative, supportive visualization here.

ACTIVITY 3, STEP SIX

Everything we do has a "pay-off." The addicted ego-self's payoff for being addicted is the "power rush" that it experiences from all of the drama that it creates. Use this space to record some of the pay-offs of the addicted ego-self and some of the pay-offs of recovery.

ADDICTED EGO-SELF'S BEHAVIOR:	PAY-OFF:
A.	A.
B.	B.
C.	C.
D.	D.
E.	E.
F.	F.
G.	G.

RECOVERY BEHAVIOR:	PAY-OFF:
A.	A.
B.	B.
C.	C.
D.	D.
E.	E.
F.	F.
G.	G.

NOTES ON STEP SIX

Write down any other thoughts, feelings, or revelations associated with Step Six.

■ **Chapter 7** ■

Step Seven: Transformation

**"HUMBLY ASKED HIM TO REMOVE OUR
SHORTCOMINGS."**

Before I begin a Metaphysical-Spiritual discussion
of Step Seven, I must say this: It is time to remove
exclusive pronouns from the Steps and program liter-
ature. The pronoun *him* refers to an outdated Judeo-
Christian concept of divinity. With the feminine
energies exploding with Power all around us, and with
the return of the Goddess, let's make room. We don't
have to burn any underwear! Just remember, we seek
balance and harmony.

Well, now that I've said that, let's move on to working Step Seven. Actually, Step Seven is really a con-
tinuation of Step Six. The original founders, the "real"
oldtimers, wisely recognized that addicts tend to over-
load themselves in their zeal for recovery. In a spirit
of wisdom and concern, they broke the recovery process down into manageable chunks. Steps Six and
Seven are helping us get ready to live life to the fullest
with the guidance of our Higher Self.

I suspect that *defects of character* and *shortcomings*
mean pretty much the same thing. I imagine that
homicidal tendencies are in another category al-
together. So, let's assume that we're going to move our

addicted ego thought and behavior patterns aside and seek the Higher Self's guidance in establishing new values that support us as wonderfully creative beings.

It is possible to have the addicted ego-self quietly (or at least as quietly as it can) and humbly turn direction of our life over to the Higher Self.

How? By reminding ourselves that the Universe allows us to make mistakes and to change and grow while we learn. For example, my addicted ego-self demands total control in every situation. When I surrender to that ego impulse, disaster inevitably follows—sort of like an old episode of *Laverne and Shirley,* only there won't necessarily be a happy ending. In my recovery, my Higher Self has taken that ego "shortcoming" and transformed it into a thirst for knowledge and a need to create. It is rare, indeed, to find me without a book. I also laugh a lot.

Everything I've ever seen, heard, smelled, touched, or known in any lifetime is still with me, recorded in my Karmic History. It is part of who I am. Why would I want any of my experiences "removed"? Instead, I have them transformed by Love into gifts that enrich not only my own life's adventure, but that of the entire planet.

Let me say once more, from a position of Metaphysical-Spiritual power: It is vital that we affirm our successes rather than just dwell on problems. There is nothing to be eliminated, only transformed. Always seek balance and harmony.

Removing and Transforming

Earlier on in this chapter, I mentioned that we do not want to "remove" or get rid of anything. Were you shocked by that? Well, this is a perfect place to further explain the difference between "removing" and "transforming."

I believe it is impossible to remove anything once we have experienced it. What we do, instead, is transform that experience from a negative debt into a positive asset. How? Well, in any number of ways. But, first, let me explain why it is impossible to remove anything.

We have several bodies—not just the physical body, which is, of course, the most easily visible body. One of the bodies we have is a Light body, which is sometimes called the Emotional body. I, personally, do not prefer to call it that, for people generally associate it with emotions such as hate, love, and so on. Instead, I call this Light body the Karmic body. It corresponds, generally, to the Physical body and is contained within the Auric Field. It is easily accessible.

The purpose of the Karmic body is this: The Karmic body records everything you ever see, touch, taste, hear, feel, think, and so on, in every lifetime you have ever lived. It is all there, recorded. The Karmic body is not connected to linear time-space; therefore, the Karmic body cannot differentiate between experiences recorded in 14th-century B.C. Egypt versus something that happened in your life last month. All of these experiences are part of your history and cannot be removed.

The challenge here is recognizing beliefs and behaviors that you identify as being unsupportive of recovery. Once you identify these behaviors, it will become obvious that they are not isolated "defects," but rather themes running through your life. The particulars simply manifest themselves differently from time to time, but the themes remain consistent.

Maybe you are thinking, Why in the world is Robert telling me all of this? I just want to quit drinking. What I'm telling you is that alcoholism is a particular manifestation of a theme running through life (indeed, many lifetimes) rather than the theme itself. And I'm telling you that the time you spend working Steps Four, Five, Six, and Seven is the perfect opportunity to begin transforming this unsupportive behavior into spiritual knowledge.

Let me give you another example of the benefit of doing this inner work in conjunction with Steps Four through Seven. In my work with clients who are making inventories, I always do a scan of their Auric Field and Karmic body. What I almost always discover is some blockage in the energy flow between the solar plexus chakra and the heart or throat chakra.

Having constrictions in the energy flow between the solar plexus and heart is sometimes encoded in the Karmic body during a lifetime where the individual died as a result of standing up for beliefs. The Karmic body, seeking to protect the person from further physical trauma (death), constricts the flow from the seat of personal power (solar plexus chakra), through to the seat of spiritual wisdom and understanding (heart chakra), or to the seat of where we speak our Truth (throat chakra). This energy constriction will prevent the person from living life to the fullest and from living his or her truth very publicly.

Perhaps it wasn't safe to speak your truth in Czarist Russia, but today it is safe to be who you are. You do not have to be protected from great visible success by an insane addiction. But, you don't want to try to "get rid of" any of your past or present personality.

Simply allow the light of freedom to begin releasing the energy constriction manifesting as "character defects" or "shortcomings," and transform these unsupportive behaviors into traits that support the most authentic expression of recovery possible. Your Higher Self will automatically accomplish this with the permission of the spoken intention of your competent ego-self (automatically, though perhaps not instantly).

As recovery progresses and as our spiritual understanding expands, we will become more aware of constrictive energy flows in the Karmic body. The Higher Self will often dissolve the constrictions without our ever being conscious of it. I am telling you this so that you don't say, "Oh, no, it is all too much . . . I can't do it."

Keep in mind that many of the spiritual concepts you may find daunting at the beginning of recovery will become "old hat" as you continue taking inventory and sharing recovery with others. My work with clients in releasing energy constrictions in the Karmic body continually deepens my appreciation of how our Higher Selves transform limitation into infinite possibility.

One thing you might want to do is find a time and place where you can have quiet and privacy. Sit comfortably with your palms facing upward. If you are familiar with *mudras*, connect the end of the thumb to the tip of the middle finger on both hands. Breathe normally. In your imagination (mind's eye), see your Higher Self seated in front of you. This Being of Light is your true spiritual essence, quite beyond any limitation of time-space.

After you have greeted your Higher Self with some sign of honor and respect (*pranam*—that is, touching forehead to ground), ask your Higher Self to bathe your Karmic body with the healing light you need most right at this moment. As that frequency permeates your Karmic body, know that you are being prepared to walk your Path in a powerful, balanced, and harmonious way. The fire of the Higher Self's Light will transform any impurities (defects of character) into spiritual treasure (strength, hope, and spiritual awakening).

Spend as much time as you wish in this meditation with your Higher Self. When you have finished, thank your Higher Self (pranam), and pull your attention back to your outer awareness.

When you see how your Higher Self transforms "shortcomings" and "defects of character," you will

STEP SEVEN: TRANSFORMATION

appreciate the treasures you possess that you could never have gotten any other way. Why, then, would you want to get rid of or "remove" the raw material that brought you those treasures? Obviously, you wouldn't. Keep in mind that even though this meditation is given in Step Seven, once you begin working Five, Six, or Seven, I believe the meditation is appropriate. There will be more about transformation in chapter 13, "Creating a Sacred Space."

SUGGESTED AFFIRMATIONS

You might wish to recite these affirmations on a daily basis while working Step Seven.

- I AM A (WO)MAN OF POWER.

- TODAY, I AM IN RECOVERY.

- ALL MY ADDICTED EGO-SELF LIMITATIONS ARE NOW TRANSFORMED INTO SPIRITUAL GIFTS.

- I AM GRATEFUL TO SHARE MY RECOVERY WITH OTHERS.

- I ALLOW MYSELF TO MAKE MISTAKES WHILE I RECOVER.

- TODAY, I ACCEPT THE GUIDANCE AND DIRECTION OF MY HIGHER SELF.

- MY RECOVERY CONTINUES TO MAGNETIZE MY HIGHEST GOOD TO ME.

- THE MOST VALUABLE GIFT I EVER GIVE TO OTHERS IS THE LIGHT OF MY OWN RECOVERY.

- ALL IS WELL.

ACTIVITY 1, STEP SEVEN

Using the information in chapter 14 on the various ego-selves, list some of the characteristics of your Higher Self and your various ego-selves.

MY HIGHER SELF:

A.   E.

B.   F.

C.   G.

D.   H.

MY COMPETENT ADULT EGO-SELF:

A.   E.

B.   F.

C.   G.

D.   H.

MY YOUNG ADULT EGO-SELF:

A.   E.

B.   F.

C.   G.

D.   H.

(continued on next page)

MY ADOLESCENT EGO-SELF:

A.   E.

B.   F.

C.   G.

D.   H.

MY INNER CHILD EGO-SELF:

A.   E.

B.   F.

C.   G.

D.   H.

MY ADDICTED EGO-SELF:

A.   E.

B.   F.

C.   G.

D.   H.

ACTIVITY 2, STEP SEVEN

While becoming aware of unsupportive traits that can be transformed into supportive characteristics and in order to stay balanced and in harmony, list some of the things that you like about yourself RIGHT NOW. It is absolutely vital that we keep in mind our successes even in the midst of the addictive process. Continue to refer to this list as you progress in recovery.

WHAT I LIKE ABOUT MYSELF RIGHT NOW:

A.	G.
B.	H.
C.	I.
D.	J.
E.	K.
F.	L.

Explain in more detail those characteristics that make you worthy and lovable.

ACTIVITY 3, STEP SEVEN

Sit quietly in meditation. After a few minutes, when you feel centered, place your Higher Self before you. In your imagination, initiate a dialogue with this Divine Being, asking for the information most needed and most appropriate for you right now. Are there constrictions in the Karmic body that you need to be aware of? Are there unsupportive beliefs to be transformed? Is any body work needed? When you finish this meditation, record your immediate impressions here. This is an activity that could easily be done every weekend as you review the events of the previous week. Please keep a record of the information that your Higher Self brings you.

NOTES ON STEP SEVEN

Write down any other thoughts, feelings, or revelations associated with Step Seven.

Chapter 8

Step Eight: Restoration and Restitution

**"MADE A LIST OF ALL PERSONS WE HAD
HARMED AND BECAME WILLING TO MAKE
AMENDS TO THEM ALL."**

Steps Four and Eight are probably first cousins. They are definitely interrelated, and working Step Eight can teach a profound spiritual lesson: All creation is interconnected. So often people say, "When I drink, it only hurts me, so it's nobody's business but my own." Well, this is far from true.

In Step Eight, we become aware of the social dimension of addiction. The addictive process is very much like an octopus, with its tentacles reaching both near and far. It harms not only the addict, but everyone who comes into contact with him or her.

How many paintings never got painted, how many songs were never sung or books never written, how many children were never hugged, because of the insidiousness of addiction?

Step Eight is not a place to beat yourself up any more than Step Four was. However, it is the place to acknowledge that because of the inherent ego-selfishness of addiction, you might have hurt other people and would like to make amends if you possibly can.

Working Step Eight once again proves the multidimensionality and interconnectedness of every being on this planet. When we make a list people who have been harmed by our addictive process, it is no longer possible for the denial system created by addiction to function.

However, for those of us walking a path of Metaphysical Spirituality and seeking balance and harmony, it is important that we take Step Eight a bit further. After you've listed those whom your addiction has harmed and you've decided you'd like to make it up to them, sit down and make another list. At this point, write down the names of all the people you've helped or touched in a positive, supportive way DESPITE your addiction! Seek balance and harmony.

I've mentioned this process to people who have been in recovery for a while, and they are often resistant. It seems easier for them to use the old "sin versus grace" model, which means that people's primary orientation tends to lean toward the negative. Left to their own devices, people will always choose bad (sin) over good. The only time people would ever accept good is when good is imposed by an outside source (God) and is an unearned gift (grace). The good would not be something we deserved, but rather something bestowed at the whimsy of an often fickle deity. This model leaves us in constant need of salvation and causes us to perpetually question our worthiness. Even though this model represents standard, orthodox Judeo-Christian dogma, it is a fairly primitive understanding of humanity's relationship to divinity.

This "sin versus grace" model of relating to Spirit

is directly opposed to that of Metaphysical Self-Empowerment. Personally, I have moved beyond "sin versus grace" in my philosophy, spirituality, and my recovery. However, even though I reject this model, I have no problem with anyone working the Steps however they need to. For me, it just seems so negative and one-sided to deny the good things that I have accomplished even in the midst of my addiction.

On a personal level, this is one of those places where my Metaphysical Spirituality really empowers me. It is impossible for me to be a victim or a victimizer when I'm realizing that addictive processes, when understood from a position of power, are simply vehicles that can transport us from one place to another, from confusion to centeredness. To define myself by that addictive process would be like saying "I am a Toyota" or "I am a Ford" simply because that is the vehicle I drive.

So, how long do you need to spend on Step Eight? Well, I suggest giving yourself several weeks to achieve a healthy balance between the folks you've harmed and the folks you've blessed. Perhaps six months down the line you may remember something else to add to your Eighth Step. That is perfectly normal. Recovery is an ongoing process, not a one-time event. Take your time.

The Communal Nature of Recovery

At this point, it would be wise to expand on the communal nature of the addictive process and recovery.

We've all heard the expression: "I can do whatever I want as long as it doesn't hurt someone else." But, what about hurting yourself? We all have others in our lives who care about us to one degree or another. Perhaps some love us deeply; maybe others are casual acquaintances whose concern is fairly limited. No matter how informal our relationship to another might be, I just don't see how we can hurt ourselves without hurting someone else. When you hear that a stranger has committed suicide, does that event not, in some way, hurt your heart? That suicide victim might have thought that his or her act would not have had a bearing on anyone else, yet total strangers are hurt. Why? Because we are not alone on this planet. We are all connected. We are all part of a community, and all of our acts affect others.

We are members of microcommunities and macrocommunities. Some of the microcommunities to which we belong are biological family, extended family, social and religious organizations, employment arenas, and 12 Step groups. Some of the macrocommunities include nations, states, provinces, social and religious organizations, and so on. Notice that some groups are both micro and macro in nature.

When we are submerged in the addictive process and our lives manifest all the insanity and confusion inherent in addiction, it is impossible for us to prevent hurting the other members of the microcommunities to which we belong. If our behavior is out of control, how can our family be healthy and sane? And, if our families are not able to function sanely, how can the nation function sanely? If the families (microcommunities) are dysfunctional, so will the nation (macrocommunity) be. The good news here is that when the individual members of the family begin telling the truth and recovering from the insanity of addictive processes, that energy will be projected into the community at large.

Your recovery as an individual will affect your family, your co-workers, and your fellow citizens. Therefore, when I work with clients who are working their Eighth Step, I insist that they also "MAKE A LIST OF ALL PERSONS I HAVE ENRICHED AND BECOME WILLING TO ACCEPT THANKS FROM THEM ALL."

As I mentioned previously, many of my clients resist making a list of the people they've helped because there seems to be an unspoken, unwritten assumption that they have been dirty, rotten scoundrels who've never accomplished anything worthwhile. Therefore, until I insist that they create a balanced list, they spend all their time beating themselves up for hurting others.

Sure, we've all hurt other people. But we've also helped some. I am convinced that many people relapse because they were never able to appreciate the gifts they gave to others. We don't have to wait until the 12th Step to begin sharing with those around us!

Achieving Balance

There is a lot written about dysfunctional families, but there is one additional issue even more basic: the

101 ▪

dysfunctional individual. The opposite of the dysfunctional individual in the midst of his/her addictive process is the recovering individual walking in balance and harmony. It seems to be impossible to move from the insanity of addiction into recovery without balanced mental, emotional, and spiritual health. You cannot make lists recounting your negative behavior and expect to achieve balance; you also need to make lists of your admirable traits, as well. Even if all you can come up with is "Sometimes I comb my hair," at least, this is something positive to counteract, "I stole money from Uncle Joe."

When I first began my recovery, I could not see one positive, supportive thing I'd ever done, yet I compiled long lists of my failures and negative behavior. If I'd seen this book way back then, I probably would have laughed at the concept of balance and harmony. I would have reacted in the same way that many of my clients do today when I guide them in inventory. However, as soon as they experience how well a balanced approach works and how wonderful recovery feels, it is hard for them to slow down and enjoy the process more. So, I do understand how looking at the Steps differently can be threatening. I only ask that you take this information into your heart and ask your own Inner Knowing about its validity for your path. All the information you need is contained within your own Inner Knowing.

As you write out your Eighth Step, please keep your notes at hand. Make an Eight Step folder, or keep an Eighth Step chapter in your journal. Continue to watch your recovery expand and grow.

SUGGESTED AFFIRMATIONS

You might wish to recite these affirmations on a daily basis while working Step Eight.

- I AM A (WO)MAN OF POWER.

- I BLESS ALL WHO ADD TO MY EXPERIENCE OF RECOVERY.

- I HONOR MY PATH BY HONORING THE PATHS OF OTHERS.

- I FORGIVE AND RELEASE ANYONE WHO HAS HARMED ME.

- I FORGIVE MYSELF FOR HARMING ANYONE ELSE.

- I LOVE MYSELF.

- MY RECOVERY ENRICHES MY FAMILY, MY FRIENDS, MY CO-WORKERS, AND MY FELLOW CITIZENS.

- I AM GRATEFUL TO SHARE MY EX- PERIENCE, STRENGTH, AND HOPE WITH ANYONE SEEKING RECOVERY.

- ALL IS WELL.

ACTIVITY 1, STEP EIGHT

Take some time to visualize the support you would like to receive from a sponsor. Now, write those things down, and refer to your list often as you work with your sponsor. Remember, you may change sponsors if you feel unsupported and unnurtured.

CHARACTERISTICS OF MY IDEAL SPONSOR:

A.   E.

B.   F.

C.   G.

D.   H.

My idea of a productive, supportive relationship with my sponsor is:

ACTIVITY 2, STEP EIGHT

This activity will give you a quick "karmic tune-up." If there are any resentments you find yourself holding on to, think about how you could begin releasing them. Do you resent a family member? A spouse? A neighbor? A co-worker? Why? Explain how you can transform this weakness into a recovery strength in Step Eight.

ACTIVITY 3, STEP EIGHT

"What I do is nobody's business as long as it is legal and doesn't hurt anyone else." We hear this statement fairly often, but is it true? Are we really so isolated that our actions have no effect on those around us? I don't think so. But, take some time to decide for yourself. Explain how your actions have touched others and how their actions have had an effect on you.

MY ACTIONS: EFFECT ON OTHERS:

A.   A.

B.   B.

C.   C.

D.   D.

OTHERS' ACTIONS: EFFECT ON ME:

A.   A.

B.   B.

C.   C.

D.   D.

NOTES ON STEP EIGHT

Write down any other thoughts, feelings, or revelations associated with Step Eight.

■ **Chapter 9** ■

Step Nine: A Balancing Act

**"MADE DIRECT AMENDS TO SUCH PEOPLE
WHEREVER POSSIBLE EXCEPT WHEN TO DO
SO WOULD INJURE THEM OR OTHERS."**

When we've completed Step Eight and listed the people we'd like to make amends to, it is time to translate that desire into action in our outer awareness.

I believe that the most wonderful restitution we could ever make to anyone would be the example of a balanced and harmonious life. That, after all, is one of the spiritual goals of our incarnation on Earth.

When we speak of amends in connection with recovery, the obvious examples stand out; the less obvious, or subtle ones, are not so readily apparent. For example, if we've taken another's property, we can return it. If we've broken our word, we can apologize and try to be more truthful in the future. Making direct amends, of course, means that the person who needs our attention gets it, not their parents or sister or Uncle Phil.

By the time recovery reaches Step Nine, a stable and focused set of values has been put into place. Using Metaphysical Spirituality, you don't need to evaluate in terms of "good" or "bad," for this process usually requires that someone be "right" and someone "wrong."

YOUR COMPANION TO 12 STEP RECOVERY

Rather, our values are based on what is supportive of who we are as Beings of Power. We will make amends in recovery because that action supports us in balance and harmony, not because we are afraid of being punished if we don't. And, again, this is a radical departure from the old fear-based Judeo-Christian approach where we "behaved" because we didn't want to go to hell!

Another very important point to consider, and one that is usually overlooked, is this: "Would injure them or others" also includes you! If making direct amends would cause *you* harm, then don't do it. Being a martyr will only add more fuel to the fire of the addictive process.

Does this mean that you don't have to make amends at all if to do so would injure others or yourself? Absolutely not! It simply means that you make indirect amends in a way that would protect the privacy of anyone who might be harmed. If there is any doubt in your mind about making amends, about how or when or to whom, then find time to sit quietly. Breathe deeply three or four times. Then, in your imagination, pull out your Higher Self directly in front of you. When you see this Being of Light, simply ask that the information you need be channeled to your outer awareness in a way that serves your recovery and in a way that serves the entire planet.

As this information flows into your conscious outer awareness, thank your Higher Self and declare your intention. Your declaration could go something like this: "I declare that I am a servant of the Light. I claim this time to bring Light and Healing to myself and anyone who needs healing from the confusion of my addicted ego-self. Healing energy now flows all through me and all around me. This healing energy now flows to whoever needs and desires it! I am a person of Power, and all is well."

In Step Nine we can also see ourselves actually manifesting the Metaphysical Law of Karma. We take responsibility for our actions and their consequences. This is not reward and punishment! It is quite simply balance and harmony.

Karma represents the various ego-selves and the Higher Self seeking balance and harmony. Karma is never the "eye for an eye" concept that many, from their fear, speak of. Metaphysical Spirituality is about liberation from the fear-based and imperfect understanding of the past. Step Nine is one of those way stations on the journey of recovery where we can release and transform old patterns and come more and more into our own Power. There is no need to rush the working of Step Nine. Take your time and meditate, reflect, and write about your ideas. There is no "right" way to work the Steps. You are free to tailor any of these suggestions to fit your circumstance and situation.

Making Amends

When you are considering how to go about making the actual amends, it is important to acknowledge the communal nature of the recovery process. You might consider volunteering your talents and time to an organization whose philosophy you support, or try to think of something else you could do that would be of benefit to the community at large.

You may, of course, be working on making amends to specific individuals while you commit yourself to some type of community service. You will probably want to involve your sponsor in the process of deciding how to make amends. After all, your sponsor will have been through this process and will be aware of the pitfalls to avoid (if you've got a good sponsor).

Timing is a very important consideration, too. From my own experience, I have learned that it is wise to avoid making amends during holidays, especially Christmas. Even with all the emphasis on peace and love, there is still a tremendous amount of stress and tension connected with the holidays. So, you see, little hints like this are what you need to elicit from your sponsor while you work your Ninth Step. This is one of those stages in recovery where you need to walk very carefully. If there is any doubt in your mind, go back to the meditation earlier in this chapter and ask your Higher Self. The Knowing is always residing there within you.

SUGGESTED AFFIRMATIONS

You might wish to recite these affirmations on a daily basis while working Step Nine.

- I AM A (WO)MAN OF POWER.

- I NOW RESTORE ANYTHING THAT NEEDS RESTORATION.

- I HONOR ALL THE COMMUNITIES OF WHICH I AM A PART.

- TODAY I COMMIT MYSELF TO TOTAL RECOVERY.

- I AM A DIVINE EXPRESSION OF SPIRIT IN PERFECT PHYSICAL, MENTAL, EMOTIONAL, AND SPIRITUAL HEALTH.

- ON A DAILY BASIS, I MOVE MORE AND MORE INTO MY POWER.

- I FREELY SHARE MY RECOVERY WITH NEWCOMERS.

- TODAY I ACKNOWLEDGE MY STRENGTHS AND WEAKNESSES IN BALANCE AND HARMONY.

- TODAY I EMBRACE MY HUMANITY AND MY DIVINITY.

- ALL IS WELL.

ACTIVITY 1, STEP NINE

Retain these lists as a valuable source of ideas for your future recovery. This activity will be very helpful to you when serving as a guide (sponsor) for others beginning the recovery process.

INNOVATIVE IDEAS ABOUT MAKING DIRECT AMENDS:

A.   F.

B.   G.

C.   H.

D.   I.

E.   J.

INNOVATIVE IDEAS ABOUT MAKING INDIRECT AMENDS:

A.   F.

B.   G.

C.   H.

D.   I.

E.   J.

ACTIVITY 2, STEP NINE

It is important to keep reminding ourselves that accepting responsibility is empowering and that blame is disempowering. Spend some time in meditation, and then record what you have determined are some of the major differences between blame and responsibility.

WAYS IN WHICH MY COMPETENT ADULT EGO-SELF ACCEPTS RESPONSIBILITY:

A.   F.

B.   G.

C.   H.

D.   I.

E.   J.

WAYS IN WHICH MY ADDICTIVE EGO-SELF BLAMES ME OR OTHERS:

A.   F.

B.   G.

C.   H.

D.   I.

E.   J.

ACTIVITY 3, STEP NINE

This is another wonderful, meditative activity. As you've done in previous activities, bring your Higher Self out in front of you. In a dialogue with your Higher Self, ask to be given several spiritual goals for your present incarnation, and then write them down here. Next to each, write a few sentences about how your addictive process and recovery are connected to each goal. You can even peer into the future and imagine how recovery from the addictive process results in the manifestation of spiritual goals. Please have fun with this activity.

SPIRITUAL GOALS:

A.

B.

C.

D.

E.

NOTES ON STEP NINE

Write down any other thoughts, feelings, or revelations associated with Step Nine.

Chapter 10

Step Ten: Consciousness

"CONTINUED TO TAKE PERSONAL INVENTORY, AND WHEN WE WERE WRONG, PROMPTLY ADMITTED IT."

In Step Four we began making a personal inventory, and in Step Five we became aware of the ego issues that kept us from experiencing balance and harmony. Step Ten is a combination of Steps Four and Five, a process (not an event) that is ongoing.

As I have mentioned previously, as one who follows a path of Metaphysical-Spiritual Power, I am not comfortable using the word *wrong*. If I am "wrong," then someone else has to be "right," and if I am "right," someone has to be "wrong." This process can lead to all sorts of imbalance: self-righteousness, judgment, blaming, fault finding, gossip and, ultimately, resumption of the addictive process.

How can the resumption of the addictive process be avoided, and how can you work the Tenth Step on an ongoing basis? Well, you can simply approach it metaphysically! I continue to assess my life, my actions, and my words in terms of my Highest Good and service to others and the planet (metaphysical inventory). When I start to indulge in fear-based ego behavior, I acknowledge it right away to myself and whoever else is involved. It is no big deal, really.

My greatest challenge has been finding people in the program who speak the same spiritual language I do. It is not that we aren't looking for the same thing. Just about everyone who comes to the program is seeking recovery, so we have more in common than we suspect, sometimes. However, I still enjoy discussing metaphysics with folks who are on that wavelength.

If you leave the old fear-based systems behind, both the old beliefs and the old vocabulary, then there is the possibility of establishing a base of power. It doesn't have to be "us against the world" and always trying to decide who is "right" and who is "wrong." Actually, the old religious system sets us up to expect faults and "wrong-doing."

So, find someone who shares your vocabulary, philosophy, spirituality, and world view. I am not implying that you have to agree with each other on every issue, but only that you understand what the other person means and that you respect and honor each other's beliefs.

I know how important it is for me in my recovery to have friends who help process my personal inventory and who give positive, supportive feedback. This, again, underscores the interconnectedness we share among ourselves and the multidimensionality of our personal recovery and the evolution of the planet.

One more thing before we leave this discussion of Step Ten and, again, this is a personal observation gleaned from my own recovery process. Today, I really enjoy saying "I apologize" or "I'm sorry" when I realize I've done or said something hurtful.

For me, it is a great relief not having to be "right" or "wrong." Saying, "Oops, I'm sorry" is my declaration of independence from the tyranny of my addicted ego-self. It frees me from having to resent myself for making a mistake or from having to resent others for being aware of my mistakes. You see, if I hurt you and am too stubborn to apologize, I know that you are aware of my stubbornness. Then, I begin resenting you because you know that I'm stubborn and not perfect! This behavior is the first ingredient in the recipe for insanity.

Conversely, when I say, "Gosh, I'm sorry I did that," I honor you by acknowledging that I value our relationship enough to heal any breach. I also show that I honor myself through my commitment to speak the truth.

Some people have trouble stating "I'm sorry" because they see "sorry" as meaning "no good." That is not the original meaning of that phrase, and it certainly is not how I intend it. "I'm sorry" means "I feel sorrow or regret," nothing more. In fact, in Spanish we say *lo siento*, which means "I feel it,"—"it" implying sorrow or regret. So, I don't believe we dishonor or disempower ourselves by saying "I'm sorry." But, if you feel uncomfortable with that phrase, find your own empowering way of allowing yourself to acknowledge regret.

SUGGESTED AFFIRMATIONS

You might wish to recite these affirmations on a daily basis while working Step Ten.

- I AM A BEING OF LIGHT.

- I NOW MANIFEST MY PERSONAL POWER FOR MY HIGHEST GOOD AND THE HIGHEST GOOD OF ALL AROUND ME.

- I HONOR MY CONNECTION TO ALL AROUND ME.

- I ACCEPT RESPONSIBILITY FOR MY RECOVERY.

- WHEN I HURT OTHERS, I QUICKLY ACKNOWLEDGE MY REGRET.

- EVERY DAY, MY EGO-SELVES BECOME MORE INTEGRATED INTO MY RECOVERY.

- THE SPIRITUAL PRINCIPLES THAT GUIDE MY LIFE ARE ALWAYS SUPPORTIVE OF MY RECOVERY.

- EVERYONE'S RECOVERY ENRICHES MY RECOVERY.

- ALL IS WELL.

ACTIVITY 1, STEP TEN

List below some recovery resources. Write down names and phone numbers of people or organizations that you can call upon (or help others call upon), rather than indulge in the addictive process.

1. COMMUNITY ORGANIZATIONS:

   A.

   B.

   C.

   D.

   E.

2. SPONSOR'S
   NAME:

3. PROGRAM FRIENDS:

   A.

   B.

   C.

   D.

   E.

   F.

   G.

ACTIVITY 2, STEP TEN

Take some time to envision yourself as a role model for others as you progress through your recovery.

In what areas do others look to you for guidance?

A.	E.
B.	F.
C.	G.
D.	H.

What do you feel capable of giving these people?

A.	E.
B.	F.
C.	G.
D.	H.

What are some of your thoughts about becoming a role model?

ACTIVITY 3, STEP TEN

Can you think of anything in particular that usually causes you to "react" rather than "act" from a place of personal power? List both reactions and actions here. Spend some time thinking about how differently you manifest your power when you "act" from a place of balance. Write down some of these thoughts so you can review them later in case you find yourself slipping into resentment.

I REACT AND FORM RESENTMENTS WHEN:	I ACT FROM A PLACE OF BALANCE AND PERSONAL POWER WHEN:
A.	A.
B.	B.
C.	C.
D.	D.

My life of recovery flows so smoothly when I act from a place of Personal Power. For example,

NOTES ON STEP TEN

Write down any other thoughts, feelings, or revelations associated with Step Ten.

Chapter 11

Step Eleven: The Higher Self Connection

**"SOUGHT THROUGH PRAYER AND MEDITA-
TION TO IMPROVE OUR CONSCIOUS CONTACT
WITH GOD AS WE UNDERSTOOD HIM, PRAYING
ONLY FOR KNOWLEDGE OF HIS WILL FOR US
AND THE POWER TO CARRY THAT OUT."**

Step Eleven is another one of those places in the program where Metaphysical Spirituality is dramatically different from traditional religion. But, before discussing the metaphysical working of the step, I will define the following terms: *Prayer, God, Will,* and *Power.*

Prayer is the flow between the Higher Self and the quieted ego-selves. It is a connection with our own Inner Knowing. Prayer for the metaphysically oriented is not going with hat in hand, eyes cast downward, asking some fickle, easily offended deity for a favor. (If you thought in those terms, you probably wouldn't have gotten past chapter 1 of this book!)

God is the creative force that brings Itself and everything into being. We are all God. The animals, the plants, the stones, the stars are all God. And, as I wrote earlier, I prefer the term *Spirit,* as too many of us have been hurt by fundamentalists using "God" to beat people up. I have no problem using or releasing the word *God,* yet I am conscious that my every orientation is toward Spirit, a constant quest for enlightenment.

Will is the agenda we have in recovery. It is composed of our intentions, interests, talents, knowledge, and our hierarchy of values. It is something that is unique to the individual. Will is not something that "God" has for us and which is often in opposition to what we want. That is an OLD AGE concept that no longer serves us. Let it go, because WE ARE GOD! WE ARE SPIRIT!

Power is knowledge of the relationship between the ego-selves and the Higher Self. Power is balance and harmony between our outer awareness in the material world and our spiritual knowing in the inner realms.

Once more, I wish we could eliminate the use of masculine pronouns for Spirit, or at least use feminine pronouns for Goddess-Her will, and so forth. The old patriarchal system is crumbling. Anyone who sits quietly in meditation can feel the Mother energies welling up from the Earth. So, let us get on with the program!

Step Eleven, then, for a person of power who is walking a path of Metaphysical Spirituality, is where the previous ten Steps come together as a whole. It is where the frequencies of recovery are manifesting themselves as balance and harmony in our outer awareness. Step Eleven is where we use meditation, affirmations, spiritual reading, journaling, and so on, to live consciously connected to Spirit. This connection becomes so primary or fundamental that our goals in life are always revolving around our inner knowing and the harmony we exhibit. Step Eleven is also a wonderful opportunity to stop and smell the roses. Recovering people have a tendency to be overly serious. So, sit back, sip some lemonade, and enjoy the progress you've made so far! Relaxing is an important part of recovery. Celebrate the harmonious balance you have achieved between your ego-self and your Higher Self, as well as with Spirit. Take time to laugh. Please, walk on the grass! The park was put there for your enjoyment, not just to be cautiously admired from a distance. There are more suggestions on celebration in chapter 13, "Creating a Sacred Space."

SUGGESTED AFFIRMATIONS

You might wish to recite these affirmations on a daily basis while working Step Eleven.

- I AM A (WO)MAN OF POWER.

- MY INNER AND OUTER LIVES ARE IN PER-FECT BALANCE AND HARMONY.

- TODAY I AM TUNED IN TO THE GUIDANCE FLOWING FROM MY HIGHER SELF.

- ALL MY WORDS AND ACTIONS ARE IN HARMONY WITH SPIRIT'S WILL FOR ME.

- I NOW BLEND THE MASCULINE AND FEMININE ENERGIES INTO A HARMONIOUS WHOLE.

- I KNOW THAT SPIRIT'S WILL FOR ME IS THAT I BE HAPPY.

- ALL IS WELL.

ACTIVITY 1, STEP ELEVEN

Be aware of some of the "small things" that can make a difference to those with whom you come in contact. For example, are you aware of how much your smile, a sincere compliment, or an encouraging word can mean to others? Here's an opportunity to list some of the ways that you bring joy to others.

A.   G.

B.   H.

C.   I.

D.   J.

E.   K.

F.   L.

Explain how you feel about the reactions of your friends/family to the great achievement of your recovery. How do *you* feel about it?

ACTIVITY 2, STEP ELEVEN

Now, spend some time writing down a few of the "small things" that can make a positive difference for you, personally. It could be a new wallet, some fancy nail polish, a new book, a weekend trip, and so on. It is important to fill up the time you once devoted to the addictive process with elements that now support your new life. Have fun.

A.   G.

B.   H.

C.   I.

D.   J.

E.   K.

F.   L.

What is a typical day like for you in recovery? How do you feel at the end of the day?

ACTIVITY 3, STEP ELEVEN

There have been several opportunities in this book for you to consciously connect with your Higher Self. I have made this contact with my Higher Self the foundation of my recovery. I love talking about my spirituality and the beneficial information that I receive from my Higher Self. Take advantage of this space to record what *your* conscious contact with your Higher Self is like. I'm sure that this is information you will enjoy sharing with others. Please keep it handy.

Conscious contact with my Higher Self is:

NOTES ON STEP ELEVEN

Write down any other thoughts, feelings, or revelations associated with Step Eleven.

Chapter 12

Step Twelve: Sharing the Harvest

**"HAVING HAD A SPIRITUAL AWAKENING AS
THE RESULT OF THESE STEPS, WE TRIED TO
CARRY THIS MESSAGE TO ALCOHOLICS, AND
TO PRACTICE THESE PRINCIPLES IN ALL
OUR AFFAIRS."**

On a personal level, the most significant thing about
Step Twelve is that it made the social dimension of
recovery so readily apparent to me. Just as the addictive process touched others, so does recovery! Step
Twelve is about concern for others. When we see how
our recovery can inspire others on the path to wellness, it is another incentive for our own balance and
harmony. So, dis-ease and wellness are not something
that is "my own business." Rather they have a profound effect on those around us.

Service to our fellow human beings is the hallmark
of the Twelfth Step. This service can be through a 12
Step fellowship, a spiritual organization, or some
other way of your own choosing. What is vital is that
we share our experience, strength, and hope in ways
that serve to heal others and ourselves.

Experiencing a spiritual awakening, just like being
in recovery, is not a one-time event. It is not compar-
able to "getting saved." A spiritual awakening is a

lifelong process that evolves and grows along with life's ups and downs. It becomes a part of the ebb and flow of life on this planet, so that the focus of recovery is always here, not off in heaven after we die. We enjoy recovery here and now, where we are and while we're alive.

Earlier on, when making amends, we spoke about recovery moving from the individual, out into the microcommunities of which the individual is a member, then out into the macrocommunities. Recovery, like addiction, is much like an octopus whose tentacles extend outward. So, the foundation we began laying much earlier in recovery is now being built up by the daily practice of these spiritual principles in all our affairs. We're putting these spiritual principles into practice, not just in 12 Step meetings, but in our personal relationships, our careers, our hobbies, and in every facet of our lives.

When your recovery reaches this stage, there will probably be many newcomers looking up to you for guidance and inspiration. This will be that special time when you can give back some of what you've received.

SUGGESTED AFFIRMATIONS

You might wish to recite these affirmations on a daily basis while working Step Twelve.

- I AM A (WO)MAN OF POWER.
- I SHARE MY RECOVERY IN WAYS THAT EN-RICH MY 12 STEP FELLOWSHIP.
- TODAY MY RECOVERY IS A PART OF THE HEALING OF THE PLANET.
- I AM HAPPY, WHOLE, AND COMPLETE.
- I EXPERIENCE BALANCE AND HARMONY IN EVERY AREA OF MY LIFE.
- I ENJOY MY 12 STEP WORK WITH NEWCOMERS.
- I AM A POSITIVE INFLUENCE DURING THE RECOVERY OF OTHERS.
- ALL IS WELL.

ACTIVITY 1, STEP TWELVE

Think about the ways that you can be of service to those with whom you attend meetings. List them here.

A.   D.

B.   E.

C.   F.

List some of the microsystems to which you belong and the ways in which your presence enriches that microsystem.

A.

B.

C.

Now, do the same for the macrosystems to which you belong.

A.

B.

C.

ACTIVITY 2, STEP TWELVE

List some attributes that would make you a good sponsor. Are any of these strengths present in your life through transformation of "weaknesses" or "defects"?

PERSONAL STRENGTHS AS A SPONSOR:

A.   D.

B.   E.

C.   F.

FORMER "DEFECTS" THAT MY HIGHER SELF HAS TRANSFORMED INTO STRENGTHS:

A.   D.

B.   E.

C.   F.

Now, think about (and write down) the parts of your personal "story" that you feel would most encourage newcomers in recovery. This information will be especially helpful when you sponsor others and when you share your story in meetings.

ACTIVITY 3, STEP TWELVE

Compared to Activity 1, Step One, this activity is at the opposite end of the spectrum. Here, you are visualizing your recovery as a tree with roots extending in every direction, but it is still important to maintain a personal awareness of the roots (or foundation) of your recovery.

Spend some time bringing into your outer awareness the behaviors, actions, thoughts, beliefs, and so on, that support your new life of recovery. Again, perhaps you could draw a tree, label it as your recovery, and write down the roots that stem from it.

NOTES ON STEP TWELVE

Write down any other thoughts, feelings, or revelations associated with Step Twelve.

POSITIVE "I AM" STATEMENTS

Use this page to write down powerful "I AM" affirmations that will help you during the various stages of your recovery.

 1.
 2.
 3.
 4.
 5.
 6.
 7.
 8.
 9.
10.
11.
12.
13.
14.
15.
16.
17.
18.
19.
20.

■ **Chapter 13** ■

Creating a Sacred Space

There was a time when there was no difference between the sacred and the mundane. Once we lived in ways that honored both ourselves and our neighbors as spiritual beings. We viewed ourselves as a part of Creation instead of being "in charge" of Creation. Those days are mostly in the past, even among the highly touted "native" or "indigenous" cultures.

The technological prowess of civilization has far exceeded the spiritual understanding needed to create a harmonious, balanced whole. It is a situation much like expecting a kindergarten student to fly and safely land a 747 jetliner.

On the other hand, we have some very holy people to look toward as models. These holy ones find themselves with vast spiritual knowledge and awareness in a culture that really does not value the spiritual wisdom that is offered. It is a situation much like teaching the ABCs to a hungry Great White shark. It is a dangerous undertaking, indeed . . . very delicate work.

I am including this chapter in this 12 Step recovery book because I believe that in addition to provoking insanity, the addictive process can rob us of our sense of the sacred. My clients are constantly asking me how

I've managed to create such a warm, positive, sacred environment. They tell me that they feel the difference in energy the very moment they step through my door. The first thing I explain to them is that the energy that surrounds me is not there by accident. It is an energy grid created by very specific intention. After I briefly discuss the "sacred" and the "mundane," I would like to share some of the things I do to create a sacred space. Please remember that I am sharing my truth, not The Truth. Experiment with this process, and adapt it in a way that feels right for you.

The Sacred and the Mundane

The dichotomy between the sacred and the mundane is an artificial designation. By attempting to separate the sacred from everyday life, we have dug a deep pit. It is a void we constantly attempt, unconsciously, to fill. Some of the things we try to fill it with include: alcohol, other drugs, food, sex, religion, money, politics, work, ad infinitum. Of course, it never works, but it is the nursery where addictive processes incubate.

I believe we had best let go of the compartmentalizing of spirituality and recovery. If you only desire connection to Spirit on Friday evening or Sunday morning, then you are not seeing that Spirituality is Reality. You might say, "Oh, sure, Robert, none of this is news." But you'd be surprised by the people I encounter who think spirituality is okay, but not part of the "real world." These people are slowly (sometimes, not so slowly) killing themselves through indulgence in their addictive process. Their idea of the "real world" is a sterile, hostile environment filled with ego struggle.

There is a better way. I am going to share some of my "secret recipes" for making your home, office, car, or wherever you spend time, into a special place.

I have an altar upon which are pictures and statues of my special spirit friends. Among them are Lord Krishna, Our Lady of Guadalupe, Ganesha, Shiva Natraja, and a beautiful photo of one of the greatest souls to teach in this century, Paramahansa Yogananda. Whenever I look toward my altar, whether on purpose or in passing, my heart fills with joy and love. My Spirit sings. Part of this is karmic and a result of my lifelong love affair with India. The important thing is that I've found symbols in my outer awareness that stimulate the higher chakras and compel me to choose love. Of course, Our Lady of Guadalupe is there because of my deep love for Mexico and my affinity for her people. Spirit is Spirit; God is God. No culture owns God. So, find an expression that really speaks to you, and make it a part of your altar. You have a right to do that without political hassle from anyone.

Occasionally, I put flowers on my altar. Every day I burn incense. A good friend once said that staying in my home was like living in a temple. It was one of the nicest compliments I've ever received.

Something else I do is place a special crystal above any door that opens to the outside. I periodically charge the crystal with the intention that welcomes any energy supporting who I am as a man of Power and returns to the source any energy that is unsupportive.

I also have various power objects that have come to me from different sources, including some very special objects given to me by a Tewa medicine man. These objects were intended for my use alone, and I honor that. There are also other special stones, carvings, and so forth, that I've received as presents from friends and teachers. Each of these gifts has a special energy that I respect. Each time I see one of my objects, my heart becomes connected to the person who brought that power to me.

When we consciously lay out an energy grid with crystals or other power objects and infuse that grid with the power of our focused intention, a sacred space is created. I always speak my intention aloud to create a safe, nurturing space. Our spiritual intention is very powerful. What we put out comes back to us.

I believe that my affirmational work also contributes to making my home a sacred space. And, please note that I do not have a sacred space IN my home, but my home IS a sacred space. I have special stones in the bathroom, and when I shower, I always say or sing my affirmations out loud. I encourage clients and friends to say their affirmations at this time, too. The clean water of the shower stimulates your Auric Field and lends intensity to your affirmations. Being in the shower is one of the most powerful times of your day. I get a kick out of imbuing every activity with specialness.

When I am in my vehicle, I hang a prayer feather, a crystal, and some New Mexican silver sage from my special home, Red Sand Coyote Place. Those frequencies help to make my vehicle a mini-chapel.

I am also fortunate enough to have some land (80 acres), and the land, in and of itself, is sacred. There are some very ancient shrines there, and I honor them by sprinkling cornmeal. I have also created some shrines there to honor the Keeper Spirits.

I try to infuse my commitment to Spirit into everything I do. I don't want to have a "job" and then go to "church" for an hour a week, then go back to my "regular life." My regular life is my recovery and my spirituality. When people come to my land, they consciously commit themselves to opening to Spirit and the energies there, especially when we do rituals at the sacred stone circle. I am continually amazed by the benefits that my visitors derive from being there. My land is named Red Sand Coyote Place in honor of my special teacher, Red Sand Coyote. I am currently writing a book about Red Sand Coyote's teachings, and I look forward to sharing more about him and Red Sand Coyote Place later on.

As I mentioned earlier, when we stop our addictive process, we're left with a lot of time on our hands. I have used that time to read, to listen to self-help tapes, to write out and say affirmations, to go to meetings, and to take inventory, among other things. Throughout this time, I have focused my intention on creating a sacred energy to encompass all of these activities.

I have a personality that enjoys ritual. Ritual is meant to lift us from our ordinary reality into nonordinary reality. If ritual merely reinforces ordinary reality, it has failed. In order to create sacred spaces, we must permeate and surround the mundane with sacred energy so that they become, at least to us, indiscernible. I believe it is a sign of great spiritual growth when the line between ordinary reality and nonordinary reality blurs due to centered ritual.

I am happy to share these ideas with you. I hope you enjoy creating your own sacred space.

▪ Chapter 14 ▪

Odds and Ends

Denial

Denial is an entire belief system that is a creation and manifestation of the addictive process and the addicted ego-self. In order for the denial system to work, a person can never recognize it as denial. For, the very moment it is recognized as being untrue, it is no longer effective. When a person is in the midst of their addictive process, the denial system appears to make perfect, logical sense.

When the denial system is shattered, one of two things will happen: either the individual begins recovery or the addictive ego-self creates another denial system. That is why it is so important to begin working the Steps or get into treatment as soon as the denial system cracks.

If the addicted ego-self is allowed to create and project another denial system, it will be much stronger than the cracked denial system it replaced. Just as recovery is a process that grows, evolves, and becomes more complex, so is the addictive process. It never stays the same. In a meeting, I once heard someone say, "While you are here working the Steps, your addiction is in the next room doing push-ups." Now, I'm not saying this to scare myself or you. But, I have learned to have a healthy respect for my addictive process and its ability to fool me, if I allow it.

So, it becomes clear that denial is a complex belief system based on falsehood, but nonetheless powerful because of that falsehood. It is a complex system, since the individual's denial system is always connected to the denial systems of others. None of us ever practices addiction or recovery on our own. We're always in it together, with others.

One last word about denial: When you confront someone's denial system, do it with quiet power and gentle strength.

Spirituality and Religion

Some people think I am anti-religion. This is not true. But I *am* one of those folks who seems to be very fond of spirituality and not too eager to join any organizations. Religion is usually an ethnic, politicized organization that claims to know what is wrong or right for everyone. But claiming to know the mind and will of God is not usually enough for religious organizers. They will invariably wind up attempting to impose their beliefs on everyone else by passing laws to support what they believe in and suppress what they disagree with. I think this clearly crosses over the line into politics. And few things are more dangerous than politicized religious fanatics (for example, those from the Middle East, Northern Ireland, Colorado, and so on).

On the other hand, spirituality is a joyful song within the heart. Spirit has no concern for your politics or your DNA or your bank account. You don't have to be an Indian to connect with the Earth Mother. You don't have to be a Christian to appreciate the wisdom of Jesus. You don't have to be a Hindu to benefit from chanting the names of God. If you want to get involved with religion in connection with the above, you're going to see a lot of dissension, anger, and judgment. I simply suggest that you leave religion alone during your recovery. It will make the process that much easier.

But don't get me wrong. I am not recommending that you avoid religion forever. I am only pointing out that the spiritual energy you bring into your recovery needs to be as free of political judgment as possible. I was never able to do that in a religion, so for this reason, I avoid religious organizations. But, maybe you don't have to. I honor our differences in this regard.

*Characteristics of the Higher Self
and the Various Ego-Selves*

Examine your behavior in light of the following information. Have fun identifying which of your ego-selves is manifesting at any given time. Remember that you can access several ego-selves at once.

I. HIGHER SELF

A. ALL-KNOWING	E. DIVINE
B. ALL-LOVING	F. ETERNAL
C. ALL-ACCEPTING	G. HEALING
D. ALL-SUPPORTIVE	H. WISE

II. Competent Adult Ego-Self

A. Honest	E. Intelligent
B. Concerned	F. Perceptive
C. Capable	G. Conscious
D. Sacrificing	H. Self-Loving

III. Young Adult Ego-Self

A. Committed	E. Curious
B. Striving	F. Supportive
C. Critical	G. Demanding
D. Competent	H. Self-Accepting

IV. Adolescent Ego-Self

A. Curious	E. Risk-Taking
B. Frightened	F. Critical
C. Bold	G. Ego-Selfish
D. Impatient	H. Demanding

V. Inner Child Ego-Self

A. Loving	E. Sharing
B. Cuddly	F. Ego-Selfish
C. Accepting	G. Impatient
D. Curious	H. Forgiving

VI. Addicted Ego-Self

A. Fearful	E. Demanding
B. Judgmental	F. Unfulfilled
C. Ego-Selfish	G. Suspicious
D. Tyrannical	H. Self-Hating

Judgment Versus Discernment

Judgment is when you look at situations, determine how they are, and wish they could change. Of course, you use your own personal hierarchy of values in deciding how things ought to be different.

Discernment is when you simply look at situations and see them for what they are. They don't need to be good or bad. If something supports who you are, embrace it. If it does not support who you are, then move on. This way, your hierarchy of values is focused on *you*, not on someone else.

Thought-Forms

The addicted ego-self will often express that "this is how everything must be done." It will be closed to any new ideas due to its fear of change. This "stubbornness" will manifest as rigid thinking composed of individual thought-forms. These thought-forms will usually preclude creativity and resist innovation. For example, some people think that if you're going to be spiritual, you'll wear white, all-cotton clothes and sandals, eat sprouts, and drink herbal tea. This is simply someone's idea of what "spiritual" looks like—a thought-form.

Remember, these thought-forms are merely projections from the constricted energy flow of the Karmic body. The challenge is to open up enough to see the "big picture" and to become more creative. Thought-forms come and thought-forms go. Just watch them pass.

■ **Chapter 15** ■

How to Finally Graduate from High School

I remember sitting in a meeting one day, accessing some anger and resentment. Being the good 12 Stepper that I am, I tried to determine the source of those emotions. To my surprise, I discovered that the roots of these feelings stretched back to high school. I was in my mid-30s at that time, so I was amazed that I was harboring resentment from so far back in my past. After all, I'd been in recovery for some years, I'd spent plenty of time in therapy, I'd read self-help books, and attended many workshops and seminars.

I wasn't surprised by the fact that I had anger, resentment, or issues to work on. Actually, I pretty much took that for granted . . . still do. What surprised me was where Spirit was directing me to go back and look: high school. I hadn't consciously thought about that time in my life for years. But, since I knew that Spirit and my Higher Self were asking me to go back and begin processing my unresolved "high school stuff," I did not hesitate to do so.

Beginning with that meeting and continuing on for a while, I started observing the individual and group dynamics of the group of people at the fellowship meetings I attended. I was able to pick out the "in-crowd," the "student council," the "jocks," the "nerds," the "fringe groups," the "cheerleaders," the most handsome, most beautiful, and the most likely to take an Uzi into a fast-food restaurant. So, you get the picture, right?

I was fascinated by the way in which many of us still fell into the roles expected of us. Well, that was one of the reasons most of us began drinking or drugging in the first place, was it not? However, in a 12 Step meeting, all these years later, to find myself back (at least emotionally) in high school, was disturbing, to say the least. But that was the time when I started drinking, so there was a sort of logic to it after all.

I don't know about you, but high school was not the happiest time of my life. I was terribly insecure and would have had to raise myself up to a place of even low self-esteem! I was not popular, nor on the student council. I was not most handsome. However, I made very good grades, always did what was expected of me, and I never ever got into any trouble. I remember feeling as if I were doing time in prison, and I just couldn't wait to escape from south Mississippi. I would look around me and wonder how in the world I ever wound up there. I thought that there was something terribly wrong with me. I was always asking so many questions that it made those around me uncomfortable. I wanted to know "why"! Even though I was a 12th-generation Southerner, I knew I had to get out in order to be happy. I just couldn't fit in.

I had no friends, so I spent all my extra time reading. I loved mysteries, history, geography, and foreign languages. I even read *Don Quixote* in the original Spanish of Cervantes. Now, don't ask me why I was able to do something special like read a novel in Spanish, yet have no self-esteem.

The fact is, I thought everyone was smarter, better-looking, and more talented than I. I was very frightened. Then, in the tenth grade, I discovered that alcohol made me feel different. When I drank, I had confidence. That was how my addictive process began. I didn't want to become a drunk; I just wanted to be accepted.

So, now we zoom back to the picture of me, years into recovery, needing to begin the transformation of those old high school constrictions into the spiritual gifts of compassion and understanding. One of the biggest surprises of my life came when I talked to people in the fellowship who had been the football captain, the head cheerleader, or the student council president. I discovered that they, too, had been insecure, and that what I had interpreted as self-confidence on their part had really been bravado that they prayed no one would see through. We had simply chosen different roles in which we were concealing the same issues—insecurity, and the resentment of those we perceived as secure. Even though the particulars may have varied, the theme was quite similar.

Discovering similarities with these people, where I had seen little in common before, created a special bond. Of course, being in a recovery fellowship often fosters such ties, but there was something deeper there as we explored our group dynamics together. (It is also important to note that we did this work on our own time, not during meetings.)

After I'd spent some time examining how I had brought my high school insecurities into my adult group dynamics, I began to feel more comfortable projecting myself as a man of Power. I worked on releasing from my past all the people I'd resented. I forgave myself for being invisible in high school. I forgave my teachers for not caring. I forgave my classmates for not liking me. I forgave the community I grew up in for being judgmental and rigid. I forgave my parents for never encouraging me at all.

This process of forgiving really did free me to speak up more often. I began telling funny stories, and people laughed. I noticed that I was actually becoming popular and well thought of in my 12 Step fellowships. I had really transformed those old constrictions into assets. I had gone out into the world and become successful. I had finally put all the old baggage full of insecurities behind me. I finally graduated from high school. And it felt really good!

The Last Word

There have been many times in my life when I've been accused of having to have the last word. This is one of those times.

My honest desire to keep this book simple has often been at odds with my natural tendency to talk. I've been talking since 1951, and it will be up to you to decide if I've actually said anything worthwhile or not. While writing this book, I hoped that if I left enough room for you to read between the lines, you could adapt these ideas and suggestions to your own life and recovery without having to imitate someone else. In this way, I believe that you become empowered, with the freedom to create your own recovery. I have no desire to be anyone's "guru du jour."

Friends are always entering and exiting my life. Each inscribes a unique mark on my own recovery. Sometimes, those friends have disguised themselves as insensitive bosses, thoughtless neighbors, hurtful co-workers, or inattentive waiters. Always, without exception, these people have left gifts for me as they departed.

I now offer you any gifts you may have found in these pages. Pass them along, for we only truly possess that which we freely give to others.

OM SHANTI OM

Robert Odom
Somewhere in New Mexico
1994

APPENDIX

Glossary

Addicted Ego-Self: A very limited aspect of the personality that seeks, unsuccessfully, to protect us from pain.

Addiction: The absence of freedom to make choices.

Addictive Process: A circular pattern of behavior and thoughts that continually sabotage happiness. The addictive process involves a substance such as alcohol, or a pattern such as compulsive eating.

Affirmations: Positive, supportive, self-empowering beliefs about health, wealth, happiness of life in general. Say them aloud until they become second nature.

Amends: The restoration of property, reputation, etc., in ways that are free of any harm or misunderstanding.

Anonymity: Honoring the common good and reputation of the fellowship beyond the individual members.

Auric Field: An energy projection of the Higher Self containing the Life Force, the Light bodies, and the Physical body. The frequencies (colors) of the Auric Field are constantly shifting and reacting to the stimulation of internal and external energies.

Big Book: A collection of stories and experiences of AA's first members, written in the literary style of the 1920s.

Blame: An aspect of anger that the addicted ego-self uses to focus on the faults of others instead of its own shortcomings. This needs to be released before we can accept responsibility for recovery.

Chakra: Energy centers permeating the Physical and Light bodies. The energy projected from each chakra has a unique vibration and purpose. There are hundreds of thousands of chakras. The major chakras are the root, sacral, solar plexus, heart, throat, and third eye. The crown chakra (thousand-petaled lotus) is sometimes included in the list, although the Karmic body is unconnected to it.

Control: A pattern used by the addicted ego-self to keep focus on the various particulars of addiction rather than the root causes of addiction (i.e., fear, guilt, and shame).

Core Affirmations: Affirmations that are vital to recovery, always including "I love myself," "I accept myself the way I am," and "I approve of myself."

Denial: The belief system of the addicted ego-self that allows it to continue hurting itself and others. It is based on fear, guilt, and shame, much like the need to control.

Easy Does It: Experience proves that the addicted ego-self loves being overwhelmed; take only the steps you can handle right now; be gentle and patient with your "selves."

Ego-Selves: The personality in any specific lifetime is composed of various sub-personalities: child ego-self, addicted ego-self, adolescent ego-self, competent adult ego-self, etc. These are all part of a Karmic history and not true spiritual essence.

Emotional Body: A term used by some when referring to the Karmic body.

Enlightenment: The process of bringing the ego-selves and the Higher Self into balance and harmony so that the Inner Knowing of the Higher Self guides life.

Fundamentalism: A narrow, limited view of religion, politics, or even 12 Step recovery, which is based on fear, guilt, and shame.

Higher Self: True spiritual essence that transcends the cycle of birth and rebirth; it is a spark of the Energy that creates the Universe and makes us brothers and sisters of the stars.

Inner Knowing: The secrets of the Universe contained within the wisdom of the Higher Self, easily accessible through centered meditation and a balanced, harmonious life.

Inventory: A balanced, compassionate recognition of your various ego-selves, including successes and mistakes.

Just for Today: Avoid overwhelming yourself. Deal with what you have on your plate right now, always seeking balance and harmony in the present moment.

Karma: The Universe seeking balance and harmony in the material world.

Karmic Body: The Light body that records every experience from every Lifetime. It is contained within the Auric Field, and its shape roughly corresponds to the Physical body. The Karmic body is unaware of the passage of time or the quality of space.

Karmic History: A record of everything we've ever experienced in any lifetime.

Keep It Simple: Rather than solving the mysteries of the Universe or straightening out Congress, concentrate on your own recovery process, as free of complication as possible.

Lifetime: The Higher Self expressing through the Physical and Light bodies in time-space, many times. This is often referred to as reincarnation, a bit of ancient Knowledge honored by most of the planet's population.

Macrocommunities: Larger systems composed of the individual microcommunities. Some prominent macrocommunities are nations, states, provinces, cities, political and religious groups, racial and ethnic groups, etc. Macrocommunities can only be as healthy or functional as the families that compose them.

Meditation: Listening to the Higher Self and Spirit Guides.

Meetings: Occasions when it is appropriate to share one's own experience, strength, and hope.

Metaphysical Spirituality: A belief system of individual empowerment and the interconnected multidimensionality of all Creation (everything is composed of Spirit . . . we are all God).

Microcommunities: Small groups that are a part of larger groups—for example, the family, a class, a group of office colleagues. If our microcommunities are healthy, they can only enrich the larger communities of which they are part.

Mudras: Finger and hand postures that enhance concentration and centeredness in meditation. The use of mudras stretches back over 5,000 years into antiquity.

Newcomer: Someone beginning recovery within a 12 Step milieu.

Oldtimer: Someone who has been in recovery within a 12 Step milieu for some time. These people are generally wonderful sources of inspiration. Listen to them.

One Day at a Time: Acceptance of the fact that the opportunity for personal power and growth exists only in the moment; in other words, Be Here Now.

Personal Power: The beliefs and values upon which a Higher Self-responsible life is based.

Powerlessness: The inevitable result of the addicted ego-self directing life, relationships, career, etc.

Pranam: A traditional East Indian way of showing respect to a teacher or holy person. It involves touching the forehead and palms of the hand to the ground. (If it is a r-e-a-l-l-y holy person, reach out and touch his or her foot!)

Prasad: Sometimes called Prasadam. It is food, service, poetry, music, etc., which is offered to God. It then becomes permeated with divinity. It is similar to the Christian doctrine of Transubstantiation, although the concept of Prasad is much more ancient.

Prayer and Meditation: Dialogue of the Higher Self, competent ego-selves, and Spiritual Guides, always focused on the individual's own Walk with Spirit.

Program: A term often used to refer to the 12 Steps.

Recovery: Recognition of the voice of the addicted ego-self, accepting addiction's gifts and placing control and direction of life's destiny with the Higher Self. It is the natural impulse toward holistic expression of the authentic self.

Religion: A rule-based, overly organized approach to Spirit, very often used by the fearful ego-selves to continue the cycle of addiction and to judge others.

Spirit: The divine, eternal energy that creates the Universe; our true nature.

Spirit Guides: Friends who are not in physical bodies. Their vision, beyond the dimensions of time-space, aids in our karmic-historical growth in a given lifetime.

Sponsor: A special friend and guide in the recovery process; ideally, it is someone with whom a common spirituality and vocabulary are shared.

Thought-Form: Energy projections from the Karmic body. These projections are usually limited definitions based upon the Karmic body's traumatic experiences.

Transformation: Taking a low frequency (character defect) and raising the vibration to a high level, usually projected from the heart, throat, or third eye chakras. The one-time defect then becomes a spiritual gift. This transformation is one of the main reasons for incarnating on this planet.

Twelve (12) Steps: Breaking the recovery process down into stages that are accessible and not overwhelming.

Suggested Reading

Bach, Richard. *Illusions: The Adventures of a Reluctant Messiah.* New York: Dell Publishing Co., 1977.

Casteneda, Carlos. *The Teachings of Don Juan: A Yaqui Way of Knowledge.* New York: Simon and Schuster, 1974.

Easwaran, Eknath., trans. *Bhagavad Gita.* Petaluma, CA: Nilgiri Press, 1985.

Gawain, Shakti. *Creative Visualization.* Toronto: Bantam, 1979.

Hay, Louise L. *The Power Is Within You.* Carson, CA: Hay House, Inc., 1991

——. *You Can Heal Your Life.* Carson, CA: Hay House, Inc., 1984.

Peyton, James W. *El Norte: The Cuisine of Northern Mexico.* Santa Fe: Red Crane Books, 1990.

Ram Dass. *Grist for the Mill.* Santa Cruz: Unity Press, 1977.

——. *Journey of Awakening: A Meditator's Guidebook.* Toronto: Bantam, 1978

——. *Miracle of Love.* New York: E. P. Dutton, 1979.

——. *The Only Dance There Is.* Garden City, NY: Anchor Books, 1974.

Sun Bear, et al. *The Path of Power.* New York: Prentice Hall, 1987.

——. *Walk in Balance: The Path of Healthy, Happy, Harmonious Living.* New York: Prentice Hall, 1989.

Wilde, Stuart. *Affirmations.* Taos, NM: White Dove International, 1987.

——. *The Quickening.* Taos, NM: White Dove International, 1988.

——. *Whispering Winds of Change.* Sydney: Nacson & Sons, Pty., 1993.

Yogananda, Paramahansa. *Autobiography of a Yogi.* Los Angeles: Self-Realization Fellowship, 1946.

About the Author

Robert Odom lives in both Santa Fe, New Mexico, and at his 80-acre retreat, Red Sand Coyote Place, in northwestern New Mexico. He teaches classes and workshops in self-empowerment and self-healing through Metaphysical Spirituality and 12 Step recovery, and he also works with individuals. Some of his most popular workshops are about Earth-centered spirituality and the coming Earth changes.

Robert attended school in Mississippi and Louisiana. He has a B.A. degree in history and German, and an M.Div. in theology and philosophy. However, Robert considers most of this data to be interesting, but unimportant. For, after completing school, he began his true education.

When he is not teaching workshops or classes, Robert is out in the desert and mountains surrounding Santa Fe, or at Red Sand Coyote Place. He also spends as much time as possible in southern New Mexico and northern Mexico.

Anyone wishing to correspond with the author may do so through the publisher or by writing directly to:

ROBERT ODOM
P.O. Box 6554
Santa Fe, New Mexico 87502

■

We hope you enjoyed this Hay House book.
If you would like to receive a catalog
featuring additional Hay House
books and products, or if you
would like information about
the Hay Foundation,
please write to:

Hay House, Inc.
P.O. Box 6204
Carson, CA 90749-6204

or call:

(800) 654-5126

■